The Hemmings Book of

PICKUP TRUCKS

ISBN 1-591150-11-6
Library of Congress Card Number: 2002107919

One of a series of Hemmings Motor News Collector-Car Books. Other books in the series include:
The Hemmings Book of Postwar American Independents; The Hemmings Book of Buicks; The Hemmings Motor News Book of Cadillacs; The Hemmings Book of Postwar Chevrolets; The Hemmings Motor News Book of Corvettes; The Hemmings Motor News Book of Chrysler Performance Cars; The Hemmings Book of Prewar Chryslers; The Hemmings Book of Dodges; The Hemmings Book of Prewar Fords; The Hemmings Motor News Book of Postwar Fords; The Hemmings Book of Mustangs; The Hemmings Motor News Book of Hudsons; The Hemmings Book of Lincolns; The Hemmings Book of Mercurys; The Hemmings Book of Nashes; The Hemmings Book of Oldsmobiles; The Hemmings Motor News Book of Packards; The Hemmings Book of Plymouths; The Hemmings Motor News Book of Pontiacs; The Hemmings Motor News Book of Studebakers.

Hemmings Motor News
Collector Car Publications and Marketplaces
1-800-CAR-HERE (227-4373)
www.hemmings.com

The Hemmings Book of

PICKUP TRUCKS

President and Publisher
James C. Menneto

Editor
Richard A. Lentinello

Designer
Nancy Bianco

Front cover: 1938 Ford Model 81C. Photograph by Don Spiro
Back cover: 1956 Chevrolet 3100. Photograph by David Gooley

This book compiles driveReports which have appeared in *Hemmings Motor News*'s *Special Interest Autos* magazine (SIA) over the past 30 years. The editors at *Hemmings Motor News* express their gratitude to the following writers, photographers, and artists who made this book possible through their many fine contributions to *Special Interest Autos* magazine:

Arch Brown	Bud Juneau	Bill Owens
Dennis David	John F. Katz	Don Spiro
Dave Emanuel	Michael Lamm	Alvaro Casal Tatlock
David Gooley	John Lee	Russell von Sauers
Robert Gross	Vince Manocchi	Josiah Work
Bob Hovorka	David Newhardt	Vince Wright
M. Park Hunter		

We are also grateful to David Brownell, Michael Lamm, and Rich Taylor, the editors under whose guidance these driveReports were written and published. We thank Chevrolet Motor Division, GM Design Staff and the Charles M. Jordan Collection for graciously contributing photographs to *Special Interest Autos* magazine and this book.

CONTENTS

Special Interest Autos (SIA) magazine's back issues are referred to in this book by issue number. If in stock, copies may be purchased directly from Hemmings Motor News at 800-227-4373, ext. 550 or at www.hemmings.com/gifts.

Double Play

The Utilitarian Beauty of Chevrolet's 1938 Coupe-Pickup

By Arch Brown

Photography by Bud Juneau

Stylish enough to hold its own in almost any social setting yet practical enough to haul at least a quarter of a ton of whatever cargo its owner needed to transport: This was Chevrolet's smart Coupe-Pickup.

Chevy had built a series of Roadster-Pickups, back in the Twenties; but it wasn't until 1936 that this practical and attractive, dual-purpose vehicle was offered to the public. Never as popular as its companion model, the Sedan Delivery, the Coupe-Pickup was manufactured only through the 1942 model year.

Owned by Tom Meleo, a Lindsay, California, orange grower and dedicated Chevrolet collector, this 1938 model is a pleasure to sit in, as well as a delight to behold. One slides easily onto its single seat, to find that the cushion and back-rest are both comfortable and support-ive. Leg room is entirely adequate, even for my 74-inch frame. With a little assist from the manual choke, the engine fires up readily. (There's a hand throttle on the dash panel, too, a handy device for advancing the idling speed if desired.) Of course, one hears the traditional clat-ter of the Chevrolet's overhead valves. Nobody ever said that a Chevy of this era is as quiet, say, as a Plymouth; but the noise isn't obtrusive, and once under way one is scarcely conscious of it.

The clutch engages smoothly with moderate pedal pressure. Shifts, with the floor-mounted lever, are easy if a lit-tle sloppy, and acceleration is surpris-ingly brisk—especially so, since this model is fitted with a comparatively tall 3.73:1 axle ratio. Down the road it cruises easily at 60 mph or so. We don't make a practice of driving these cars wide-open, and I'm sure the owners would react negatively if we made any such proposal; but owner Tom Meleo estimates that this one would do 75 if pushed. We had no opportunity to try it in the hills, either; for the Meleo ranch is located in the heart of California's San Joaquin Valley, and there isn't so much as an ant hill in sight. But we know from past experience with Chevrolets of this era that their 170-lbs.ft. of torque is plenty sufficient, and thus capable of handling the hills with ease.

Perhaps we should pause at this point and explain that at the time this dual-purpose machine was built, Chevrolet offered two series of passenger cars,

Originally published in Special Interest Autos #183, May-June 2001

driveReport car offers a comparatively comfortable ride, our point of reference is the competition, Ford and Plymouth, both of which came with straight front axles in 1938. Neither of them offers the soft ride of the Master Deluxe Chevy, nor does this Master model. But on the other hand, the straight-axle Chevrolets of this era corner much flatter than those equipped with "Knee Action." And the front end was more durable as well.

Steering, though it may seem heavy now that most of us are accustomed to a power assist, is really comparatively easy in relation to other cars of the late 1930s. Nor is excessive wheel winding required. About three and three-quarters turns are enough to take the wheel from lock to lock.

Brakes are excellent, at least by the standards of the time. The Standard models of earlier years had used pressed steel drums; and when braked hard from high speeds, one could almost feel the drums warp out of shape. By 1937 all Chevys came with cast-iron drums, a great improvement; and the lining area of 158.2 square inches was more than adequate.

People speak of the six-cylinder Chevrolets of 1929-62 as "Stove-Bolt Sixes," as though the same basic engine was employed throughout that long stretch of years. But the fact of the matter is that the Chevy engine was very thoroughly revised for the 1937 season, emerging as a more powerful and much more durable powerplant. Primarily the work of Edward H. Kelley, formerly of Studebaker, the new Six was slightly larger in displacement than the 1936 engine (216.5 vs 206.8-cubic-inches) and featured a rigid, 68-lb. crankshaft. Four main bearings were fitted in lieu of the previous three, yielding ten percent greater bearing surface; the stroke/bore ratio was shortened from 1.21:1 to 1.07:1; and the compression ratio was advanced from 6.00:1 to 6.25:1. Horsepower was thus increased from 79 to 85, while torque was similarly enhanced to 170-lbs.ft. Other modifications included the substitution of a gear-type oil pump for the previous vane device, as well as a much lighter flywheel.

There was a new frame, derived from that of the 1936 Standard series. Lighter yet stronger than the previous Master frame, it was of ladder-type construction with stiff box-girder siderails and four boxed cross-members. The freshly designed body was of all-steel construction, Chevrolet having finally abandoned the heavy composite wood-and-steel type that had been employed from the division's earliest days. A substantial savings in weight was thus achieved. And the troublesome Dubonnet "Knee Action" was redesigned for greater durability by Leon Chaminade,

known respectively as the Master and the Master Deluxe. Gone was the downsized Standard series of 1934-36; commencing in 1937 all Chevys used the same 112¼-inch wheelbase, and all were powered by the same 85hp engine, a stout piece of machinery of which we'll have more to say presently. Different rear gear ratios were used, however, with the Master using the 3.73 "economy" axle while the Master Deluxe was fitted with 4.22 cogs in the interest of livelier performance. About $66 separated the two lines; and for the extra money the Master Deluxe buyer received a better grade of trim and—most importantly—the Dubonnet system of independent front suspension, or "Knee-Action." In contrast, the Master line of which the Coupe-Pickup is a member, came with an I-beam front axle.

So when we tell the reader that our

another recruit from Studebaker.

The new body for 1937 was lighter, stronger, lower, and wider than before. Styling was the work of Jules Agramonte, who had been primarily responsible for the classic design of the 1934 La Salle. A particularly neat touch was a device that GM styling head Harley Earl called the "diamond crown speedline." As described by authors Langworth and Norbye, this was "just a crease in the body, starting in the valley between the front fender and engine compartment, then flowing at a sinking angle back across the cowl and onto the front door." Whatever it was, it was highly effective, and it serves to identify the Chevrolets of 1937-38.

Having changed both engine and body design for 1937, the most visible changes for '38 were a new grille and redesigned side panels for the hood. The grille, designed by Frank Hershey whose most recent assignment had been the styling of the 1934 Pontiac, consisted of

CLUB SCENE

Vintage Chevrolet Club of America
P.O. Box 5387
Orange, CA 92863-5387
818-963-0205
Dues: $25/year; Membership: 8,000

Gas filler cap located on rear passenger side.

Harley Earl called this crease the "diamond crown speedline."

horizontal, rather than vertical bars; and the side trim had the visual effect of adding length to the hood. Altogether, it was quite an effective piece of work.

But after a couple of seasons during which Chevrolet had built more cars than at any time since 1929, 1938 proved to be a recession year, with production falling almost to its 1933 level. It was cold comfort that both Ford and Plymouth fared even worse. A partial recovery was experienced during 1939, but not until 1941 would Chevrolet come within sight of its pre-Depression sales volume.

The Coupe-Pickup was intended by Chevrolet to be a true dual-purpose car. As originally offered in 1936, it was a member of the Standard series. The rear deck opening was larger than that of the business coupe, which added to the width of the cargo box but made it impossible to convert the car to a regular business coupe. But with the demise of the Standard line, the Coupe-Pickup was able to take advantage of the wider body of the 1937 Master series. Thereafter, it was delivered with both a turtleback and a box, so that with a very simple procedure it could be converted from pickup to business coupe and back again. All that was required for the conversion was to loosen a couple of bolts, slide out the pickup box, remove a small panel beneath the place where the box had stood—in effect, an access door to the spare tire—and slip the turtleback trunk lid into place. That little panel, by the way, is an exceedingly rare item, for it was often thrown away or simply left by the wayside when a tire was being changed. We know of one prominent Chevrolet collector who, having searched in vain for this panel, had to have one fabricated by a metal worker.

This particular car actually started life as a business coupe; but owner Tom Meleo learned that a friend of its original owner had a pickup box, complete with the elusive lower panel, that was not being used. And yes, the neighbor was will-

Styling of front end similar to 1938 Cadillac and Pontiac cousins.

Accessory bumper guard precludes use of crank.

WHAT TO PAY

Low	Average	High
$1,500	$5,000	$11,000

ing to part with the setup. Thus it was simple to convert the coupe to the much rarer and more desirable Coupe-Pickup.

This was in 1973, and the Chevy had seen 35 years of hard use at the hands of its original owner; so the restoration was a major undertaking for Tom Meleo. Fortunately, he is a skilled mechanic, and Chevrolets have always been his specialty. He rebuilt the engine, installed a new clutch and pressure plate, and went through the brakes—drums, lining, master cylinder, wheel cylinders, the works! The front-end assembly was completely rebuilt. The front axle had been bent, and Tom replaced it with a good used unit. Fortunately, both the transmission and rear-end assembly were found to be in good condition.

Technically, Meleo's Coupe-Pickup should have one additional leaf in each rear spring. According to Jerry Gray, of Arlington, Texas, who has made a study

specifications

illustrations by Russell von Sauers, The Graphic Automobile Studio
© copyright 2001, Special Interest Autos

56.375 inches

112.25 inches

1938 Chevrolet Coupe-Pickup

Original price $689 f.o.b. factory, with standard equipment

Options on dR car Wheel trim rings, bumper guards, white sidewall tires, passenger-side wiper, cigarette lighter, after-market wheel covers

ENGINE

Type	In-line 6-cylinder, cast en bloc
Bore x stroke	3 inches x 3¾ inches
Displacement	216.5 cubic inches
Compression ratio	6.25:1
Horsepower @ rpm	85 @ 3,200
Torque @ rpm	170 @ 900-2,000
Taxable horsepower	29.4
Valve configuration	OHV
Valve lifters	Mechanical
Main bearings	4
Crankshaft	Counterbalanced; vibration damper
Fuel system	Carter W1 single downdraft carburetor, camshaft pump
Lubrication system	Pressure to main, connecting rod and camshaft bearings
Cooling system	Centrifugal pump
Exhaust system	Single
Electrical system	6-volt battery/coil

CLUTCH

Type	Single dry plate
Diameter	9 inches
Actuation	Mechanical, foot pedal

TRANSMISSION

Type	3-speed selective, floor lever, synchronized 2nd and 3rd speeds
Ratios, 1st:	2.94:1
2nd	1.68:1
3rd:	1.00:1
Reverse	2.94:1

REAR AXLE

Type	Hypoid
Ratio	3.73:1
Drive axles	Semi-floating
Torque medium	Torque tube

STEERING

Type	Saginaw worm-and-roller
Ratio	16:1
Turns lock-to-lock	3¾
Turning diameter	38 feet, 6 inches

BRAKES

Type	4-wheel internal hydraulic, drum type
Drum diameter	11 inches
Effective area	158.2 square inches
Drum material	Cast iron

CHASSIS & BODY

Construction	Body-on-frame
Frame	Ladder type, box girder siderails, 4 cross-members
Body construction	All steel
Body type	2-passenger coupe-pickup
Layout	Front engine, rear-wheel drive

SUSPENSION

Front	I-beam axle, 36" x 1¾" 9-leaf semi-elliptic springs
Rear	Rigid axle, 49" x 1¾" 8-leaf semi-elliptic springs
Shock absorbers	1-way hydraulic lever type
Wheels	Pressed steel
Tires	6.00/16 4-ply

WEIGHTS AND MEASURES

Wheelbase	112.25 inches
Overall length	187.0625 inches
Overall width	70.25 inches
Overall height	68 inches
Front track	56.375 inches
Rear track	59 inches
Min. road clearance	8.5 inches
Weight	2,945 pounds

CAPACITIES

Crankcase	5 quarts
Cooling system	14 quarts
Fuel tank	18 gallons
Transmission	1.75 lb.
Rear axle	3 lb.

CALCULATED DATA

Stroke/bore ratio	1.07:1
Eng. revolutions/mile	2,794
Hp per c.i.d.	.393 pounds
Weight per c.i.d.	13.6 pounds
Lb. per sq. in. (brakes)	18.6

Crank-hole cover integrated into grille.

PARTS PRICES

Grille	$400
Steering box	$289
Rebuilt carburetor	$164
Starter	$140
Fuel pump	$95
Brake drums	$85
Inner and outer front wheel bearing set	$74
Engine gasket set	$52
Door mirror	$38
Set of spark plug wires	$19
Distributor cap and rotor	$16
Set of spark plugs	$9

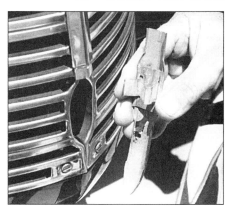

Crank-hole cover held by tension clip.

Straight-axle Master models corner flatter than Master Deluxe.

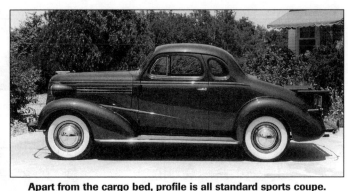

Apart from the cargo bed, profile is all standard sports coupe.

Easy engine access typical of the era.

PROS & CONS

Pros
Uncommon
Very useful
Mechanical parts plentiful

Cons
Difficult to find
Heavy steering feel
Some body panels very rare

PARTS SUPPLIERS

Bruce Horkey Wood & Parts
Rt. 4 Box 188H
Dept. SIA-183
Windom, MN 56101
507-831-5625
Bed wood and related hardware

Chevs of the 40s
2027 B Street
Dept. SIA-183
Washougal, WA 98671
800-999-2438
Chrome trim and headlight and marker light assemblies

Engineering & Manufacturing Services
P.O. Box 24362
Dept. SIA-183
Cleveland, OH 44124
216-541-4585
Reproduction sheet metal parts

The Filling Station
990 South Second St.
Dept. SIA-183
Lebanon, OR 97355-3227
800-841-6622
Repro weatherstripping, glass, floormats and interior knobs and handles

Hampton Coach
P.O. Box 6
6 Chestnut St.
Dept. SIA-183
Amesbury, MA 01913
888-388-8726
Upholstery, carpeting and panel sets

Kanter Auto Products
76 Monroe St.
Dept. SIA-183

Boonton, NJ 07005
800-526-1096
Brake and suspension parts

Mar-K Quality Parts
6625 W. Wilshire Blvd.
Dept. SIA-183
Oklahoma City, OK 73132
405-721-7925
Bed hardware and tailgates

Obsolete Chevrolet Parts Co.
P.O. Box 68
Dept. SIA-183
Nashville, GA 31639-0068
800-248-8785
Reproduction body parts, chrome trim and weatherstripping

Patrick's Antique Cars and Trucks
P.O. Box 10648
Dept. SIA-183
Casa Grande, AZ 85239
520-836-1117
Pistons, cylinder heads and engine rebuild kits for 1937-1962 six-cylinder Chevy engines

Pro Antique Auto Parts
50 King Spring Rd.
Dept. SIA-183
Windsor Locks, CT 06096
860-623-8275
Chrome trim part, gaskets and headliners

Steele Reproduction Parts
6180 Hwy 150 East
Dept. SIA-183
Denver, NC 28037-9735
800-544-8665
Reproduction weatherstripping

of this particular model, the Coupe-Pickups came from the factory with rear springs identical to those of the sedans, meaning that they had one more leaf than those fitted to the coupes. This would surely make sense if the vehicle were to be used for hauling cargo, but in Tom Meleo's case it would have made no sense to make the change; so our driveReport car retains its original springs.

Cosmetically, the little Chevy must have appeared nearly hopeless, for all four fenders were severely dented, as were the running boards, and the hub-caps and grille. It was Tom's good fortune that he was able to replace all of these casualties with new-old-stock items.

Beyond the new set of fenders, body and paint work were handled by Les Doyle of nearby Porterville, with pin-striping by Ruben of Visalia. A Hampton Coach upholstery kit was installed by Brent's Upholstery, also of Visalia. The

"...With the demise of the Standard line, the Coupe-Pickup was able to take advantage of the wider body of the 1937 Master series."

Odd handbrake was one-year-only design.

Tote box extends all the way to the back of the front seat.

Compartment for the spare tire is located under the bed.

original color had been black; but Meleo already has in his collection two black 1937 Chevys, so he went with the "Export Blue" color in which the car is displayed here. (This is a legitimate 1938 Chevrolet color, by the way, but its use was confined originally to commercial vehicles rather than passenger-cars.)

Today, Tom Meleo's Coupe-Pickup looks and runs almost like a new car. And thanks to the quality of its restoration, not to mention the fact that it is such a rare model, it is one of the most interesting and desirable of the three dozen or so Chevrolets in Tom's collection. ᏬᏝ

Chevrolet's sturdy 216.5-cubic-inch straight-six produces 85hp and 170-lbs.ft. of torque.

Basic instrument panel has 100-mph speedo.

Glovebox door cut-out for optional clock.

Lift-off panel hides spare tire compartment.

Loading the cargo bed is easy from the rear, but it is entirely inaccessible from the sides.

POPULAR IT WASN'T

We've never understood why the versatile Chevrolet Coupe-Pickup never achieved the popularity that it deserved. Unfortunately, Chevrolet was pretty sloppy about maintaining production records during the 1930s, so our information is not as complete as we might have wished. (Note that there is no record at all with respect to the 1937 model, yet we know that such a vehicle was produced.) In any case, here, as best we can put it together, is the price, weight and production table for the Coupe-Pickup:

	Price	Weight	Production
1936	535	2,760	3,193
1937	n/a	n/a	n/a
1938	689	2,945	n/a
1939	669	2,925	n/a
1940	699	3,025	538
1941	754	3,195	1,135
1942	865	3,230	206

1952 CHEVROLET HALF-TON PICKUP

By 1952 Chevrolet was selling half again as many trucks as Ford, despite the fact that the Chevy still employed the aging "stove-bolt six," while Ford offered the buyer the choice of a new, state-of-the-art, short-stroke six or, alternatively, the only V-8 then available for a light commercial vehicle.

It hadn't always been so. For years, Ford had dominated the light-truck market with its ubiquitous Model T. Catalogued as early as 1911, these practical little machines had actually been available even earlier, for a number of independent manufacturers utilized the sturdy Ford chassis in the construction of commercial units.

It wasn't until 1918, the year the company became part of General Motors, that Chevrolet got into the act. Chevy, in those days, was virtually a full-line manufacturer, building automobiles in three distinct price ranges. There was the 490, designed to compete with the Model T—though it never managed to match Ford's remarkably low price. Powered by a 171-c.i.d. overhead-valve four and fitted to a wheelbase of 102 inches, its original $490 price had grown—thanks to wartime inflation—to $685.

Next up was the Series FA. This one, selling at $995—about the price of a Dodge—had a wheelbase of 108 inches and outweighed the 490 by almost 800 pounds. Its engine, new that year, was another overhead-valve four-banger, a splasher of 224 cubic inches' displacement. And at the top of the line was Chevrolet's first V-8. Considerably more costly at $1,550 than a six-cylinder Buick, this big, 3,200-pound automobile had a wheelbase of 120 inches. Its ohv engine displaced a healthy 288 cubes.

It wouldn't have been feasible for Chevy to have used the V-8 to power a commercial line; it was too costly to build. But the 490 and the FA seemed

WILLING WORKHORSE

by Arch Brown
photos by Vince Manocchi

ideally suited to the purpose. Accordingly, for the 1918 season the company introduced two series of trucks. The first was a light delivery, based upon the little 490. It had a rated capacity of half a ton, and it sold for a modest $585. The other was a one-tonner, employing the engine and transmission of the FA, in combination with a worm-drive axle. The chassis was especially designed for this application, with a wheelbase measuring 125 inches. The price came to $1,245, a tidy sum in those days. The larger unit must have been a hard-riding brute, for although high-pressure pneumatic tires were fitted to the front wheels, the rears carried solid shoes until 1920,

(Possibly by coincidence, Ford's first one-ton truck was also introduced in 1918. And nobody has satisfactorily explained why the one-ton Chevy was designated the Model T!)

It should be noted here that Chevrolet, at that time, supplied only the chassis and cowl. Either the dealer or the customer had to contract independently for the body. Not until 1930, surprisingly

enough, did Chevy undertake to build the complete vehicle. In that year a truck body plant was established at Indianapolis, a move which resulted in a substantial savings in manufacturing costs.

Success came slowly. Just 395 commercial units were built during 1918, Chevrolet's first year as a producer of trucks. Within two years that figure had increased to 8,612, and after a severe dip during the recession of 1921, the growth continued. Production surpassed the 100,000 mark in 1927, and reached double that figure nine years later. More than 350,000 Chevy trucks left the factory in 1951. And by 1952, the year our driveReport pickup was built, there were more than two-and-a-half million Chevrolet trucks on the road.

Meanwhile, the Chevrolet passenger car line had been greatly simplified. The V-8 had been dropped early in 1919, the victim of dismal sales. It was followed into oblivion by the mid-sized car (known by then as the Series FB) at the close of the 1922 season. And from 1923 onward, Chevy concentrated exclusively upon the low-priced field. The 490 was dropped that year in favor of an improved (and much more stylish) version called the Superior, which then formed the basis for both the half-ton and the one-ton commercial units.

While the Superior represented an advance over the old 490, it still was not the sturdiest of vehicles; and the half-ton Chevrolet truck, especially, didn't enjoy the best of reputations. The chief problem was a fragile rear-end assembly which, in combination with a jumpy, leather-faced cone clutch, sometimes left the driver with a broken axle or a stripped pinion gear. Not until 1925 was a plate clutch adopted and the rear axle strengthened.

By 1927, assisted by the shutdown of Ford's facilities in preparation for the coming of the Model A, Chevrolet had

Driving Impressions

In 1952, when our driveReport truck was built, the pickup was still regarded simply as a utility vehicle, a workhorse. Amenities were few. The traditional I-beam front axle combined with the relatively firm springing to provide a ride that was (and is) stiff and somewhat choppy. No doubt it would be improved by the addition of a few hundred pounds of cargo, but the bed was empty when we took our test drive.

This particular unit is no showpiece. Its owner, graphic designer Bob Rocchio, of Newport Beach, California, uses it daily in his work and for the 40-mile round trip between his home and his studio.

Bob is the truck's second owner—or its fourth, depending on how you look at it. Purchased new by a service station operator, it was passed along successively to the man's son and then to his grandson. At that point Rocchio's son, a high school student, spotted it. Aware of his father's penchant for older Chevrolets (Bob owns a fine '51 convertible in addition to the truck), the younger Rocchio went home with the news of his discovery. A solid year of negotiation followed before the purchase was made, in 1982.

The Chevy had logged 130,000 miles by the time it changed hands. Today the figure is approaching 160,000. The engine needed some attention, so a few months after the purchase Bob gave it a complete overhaul. The paint on the cab needed only a good polish job, but Bob refinished the fenders, running boards, bed and side rails. He also fitted a set of oversize (6.50/16) tires, adding to the truck's rugged appearance.

The pickup will readily sustain a speed of 70 miles an hour, Rocchio reports, though he rarely drives it that fast. Traveling at 50 to 52 mph—and occasionally a lot slower, when he gets caught in the rush hour traffic on the Los Angeles freeway system—Bob averages 17 to 18 miles to the gallon. And he has learned not to be startled when the drivers of big 18-wheelers give him a blast on the air horn, followed by the thumbs-up sign!

We enjoyed our drive in this neat little pickup. One sits up high; visibility is superb, the more so because of the rear quarter windows. The seat is firm, supportive and roomy enough for three. Steering is comparatively light for a non-powered mechanism, thanks in part to the huge steering wheel. Acceleration is more than adequate. The column-mounted gearshift operates easily enough, though the linkage is a little sloppy. The clutch is as smooth as any we've used of late, and pedal pressure is not excessive. The truck takes the corners with aplomb, and its brakes are very effective.

There's nothing handsome about this little pickup, though its looks are somehow appealing. It is plain, almost Spartan; sound insulation, for instance, is virtually nil. But it's a stout, competent machine, one that commands respect. And it's more pleasant to drive than one might imagine!

Having read this far, the reader will have deduced that we like Bob Rocchio's Chevy pickup. Especially we appreciate:

- Its stout construction;
- The panoramic visibility;
- The unexpected roominess, even for our long legs;
- The full set of highly legible instruments;
- The comparative ease of handling;
- The flat cornering;
- The smooth operation of clutch and brakes;
- The impressive low-end torque of the engine.

All of which is not to say that this truck is perfect. For one thing, it's obvious that pickups wouldn't be in such widespread use today if they hadn't adopted independent front suspension. This one really rides pretty hard!

Beyond that, we could wish for:

- Better sound insulation;
- Less slack in the gearshift linkage;
- Slightly taller gearing, to cut the engine revolutions.

And yes, we know that the short-stroke engine of the 1952 Ford six is a more modern and efficient design. But perhaps, in a truck application, the advantage may be more apparent than real. There's something to be said for the low-speed lugging power of the old Chevy long-stroker.

Later Chevy trucks were a lot more stylish, and ultimately they became more comfortable as well. But, evaluated by the standards of its day, the '52 Chevrolet half-ton deserves a lot of respect.

*Above: Parking lamps are neatly integrated into grille design. **Right:** Spare stays clean and handy in its sidemount rather than hanging below the pickup bed with its dirt and inconvenience. **Below:** Small rectangular taillamps are a characteristic of late forties/early fifties light-duty Chevy trucks. **Bottom:** Big, bold identification on the hood.*

1952 CHEVROLET

overtaken Ford to become America's leading producer of trucks. The company slipped back to second place a couple of years later, but it was only a temporary bobble. By and large Chevy's truck operations have paralleled the phenomenal success, over the years, of its passenger car sales.

The 1928 Chevrolet light trucks featured, for the first time, four-wheel mechanical brakes. Styling reflected that of the passenger cars, and the horsepower of the little four-banger was raised from 26 to 35. There was a handsome roadster-pickup that year and a coupe-panel as well, both units derived from the passenger car bodies.

All of this, however, was no more than a prelude to 1929's big news: the introduction of the legendary stove-bolt six. By far the lowest-priced six in either the passenger car or commercial vehicle market (see *SIA #34*), the new engine displaced 194 cubic inches and developed 46 horsepower—six more than Ford's Model A. The wheelbase of the half-ton units had grown, by this time, to 107 inches, and a very attractive sedan delivery joined the line. Also new that year was Chevy's first one-and-a-half-ton truck, which served to broaden the firm's market.

The Depression, inevitably, had a devastating effect upon the entire automobile industry. At Chevrolet, passenger car production fell by 65.5 percent between 1929 and 1932, while the division's output of commercial vehicles plummeted by 69.5 percent. But the trucks recovered more rapidly than the cars, bouncing back by 1934 to 87 percent of their best pre-Depression sales. Chevrolet's passenger cars, over the

same period, recovered only 66.6 percent of their 1929 market.

Dramatic improvements were made. Hydraulic brakes and all-steel cabs were introduced for 1936, the same year that the appealing coupe-pickup joined the line. Production of both passenger vehicles and trucks surpassed their 1929 levels that year—a remarkable achievement, for the nation had not yet fully recovered from the effects of the Depression.

And for 1937 there was a brand new engine. Stronger and more powerful than the earlier six, it featured four main bearings (compared to the previous three) and a reduced stroke/bore ratio. Styling—as it had for a number of years—followed the theme of Chevrolet's passenger cars.

Something of a horsepower race had taken place among the low-priced cars and trucks, in the years just prior to World War II. In response to Ford's lively V-8, Chevrolet had advanced the horsepower of its six-cylinder engine to 80 in 1934, then to 85 in 1937, and finally to 90 in 1941. Styling, in the latter year, moved in a new direction, establishing a separate theme for the commercial units, These were ruggedly handsome vehicles, though they bore little resemblance to the contemporary Chevy passenger cars. Ford, incidentally, followed the same pattern a year later, though not quite as effectively, in the opinion of many observers.

When civilian truck production was resumed after the long wartime hiatus, Chevrolet's commercial units were virtually identical to their pre-war counterparts. But during the summer of 1947—more than a year ahead of Chevy's new, post-war passenger cars—the 1948

Above: Owner has installed this protective step plate on driveReport truck's running-boards. *Left:* Fuel tank is under cab, not the safest place to have put it. *Below:* Same body shell was used for Chevy half-tons from '48 through '54 model years.

Louis Chevrolet: You Win Some, You Lose Some!

Exactly what brought about the break between Louis Chevrolet and Billy Durant, we shall probably never know.

They were an odd combination, of course, differing in temperament and outlook, and apparently in objectives as well. Billy was a promoter who played out his life on a wide screen. Louis was an engineer, an inventor and, in his prime, one of the world's leading automobile racing drivers. (He had piled up records at every important track in the United States, and he liked to boast that the only time he was ever beaten by arch-rival Barney Oldfield was the day his car broke down.)

The two men had teamed up after Durant had lost control of General Motors, in 1910. Durant, who usually (though not always) had a pretty good sense of what would play in Peoria, wanted to capitalize on Chevrolet's racing reputation, as well as his engineering skill. Louis had no trouble with that, but evidently he and Billy had diametrically opposite ideas of what the new car should be.

Round one went to Louis. The first car to bear the Chevrolet name was a machine called the Classic Six. Big, fast, and—at $2,150—more costly than a Cadillac, it was just the sort of automobile that could be expected to appeal to a racing driver. It held little charm for Durant, however. He had his eye on the mass market, which he eventually invaded with a cheap little car called the Chevrolet 490—the very sort of machine that someone like Louis would inevitably regard with disdain.

To what extent their falling out resulted from such policy differences as this, and to what extent it was due to what Chevrolet termed Durant's "persistent interference" in his personal life, is open to conjecture. But, in any event, the break came in 1914. Legend has it that Louis stormed into Billy's office and threw his Chevrolet stock certificates on Durant's desk, with certain obscene suggestions as to what might be done with them.

The story may be apocryphal, but the

fact remains that in his later years Chevrolet found himself in modest circumstances, to say the least. He built the Ford-based Frontenac racer for a time, then manufactured high-performance Frontenac cylinder heads for the Model T. He was briefly associated with Stutz, then organized the short-lived Chevrolet Aircraft Company of Indianapolis. At one point he became involved with speedboats, and in 1925 he was the top winner at the Miami regatta.

Louis returned to the Chevrolet Division in 1936. Some sources say that he worked in public relations; others claim that he was employed on the assembly line. Either way, it must have been humiliating for him to occupy such a low-level position in the company that bore his name.

Like his erstwhile partner, Billy Durant, Louis Chevrolet was quite forgotten by that time—and broke. Ill health compelled his retirement in 1938. Three years later he was dead, at the age of sixty-two.

specifications

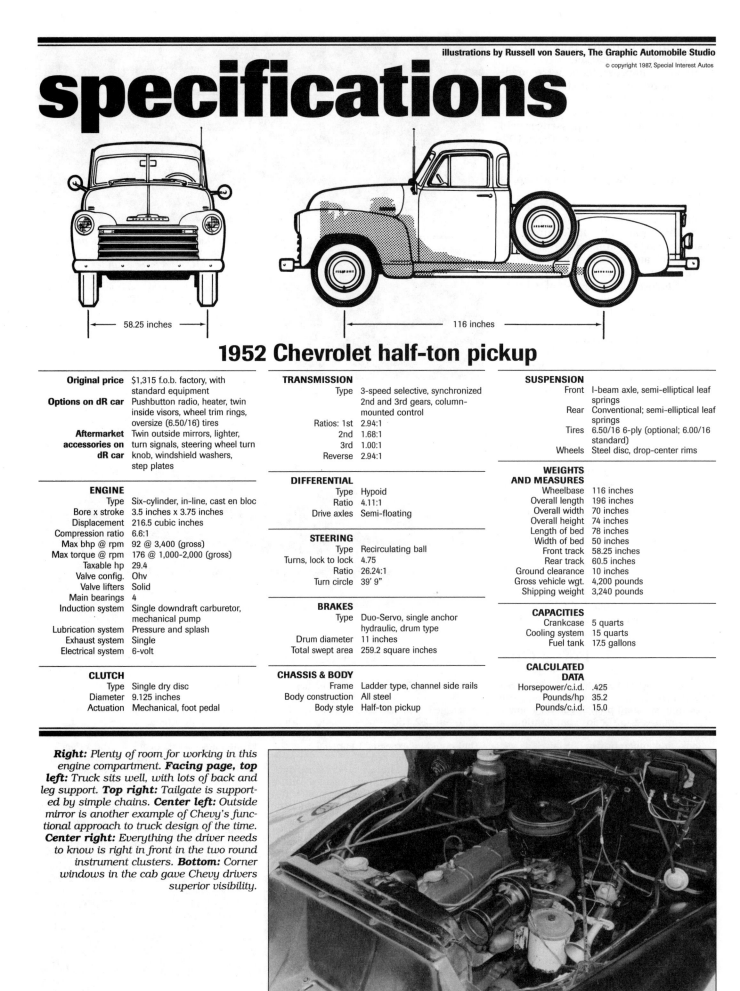

← 58.25 inches →

← 116 inches →

1952 Chevrolet half-ton pickup

Original price $1,315 f.o.b. factory, with standard equipment

Options on dR car Pushbutton radio, heater, twin inside visors, wheel trim rings, oversize (6.50/16) tires

Aftermarket accessories on dR car Twin outside mirrors, lighter, turn signals, steering wheel turn knob, windshield washers, step plates

ENGINE
Type	Six-cylinder, in-line, cast en bloc
Bore x stroke	3.5 inches x 3.75 inches
Displacement	216.5 cubic inches
Compression ratio	6.6:1
Max bhp @ rpm	92 @ 3,400 (gross)
Max torque @ rpm	176 @ 1,000-2,000 (gross)
Taxable hp	29.4
Valve config.	Ohv
Valve lifters	Solid
Main bearings	4
Induction system	Single downdraft carburetor, mechanical pump
Lubrication system	Pressure and splash
Exhaust system	Single
Electrical system	6-volt

CLUTCH
Type	Single dry disc
Diameter	9.125 inches
Actuation	Mechanical, foot pedal

TRANSMISSION
Type	3-speed selective, synchronized 2nd and 3rd gears, column-mounted control
Ratios: 1st	2.94:1
2nd	1.68:1
3rd	1.00:1
Reverse	2.94:1

DIFFERENTIAL
Type	Hypoid
Ratio	4.11:1
Drive axles	Semi-floating

STEERING
Type	Recirculating ball
Turns, lock to lock	4.75
Ratio	26.24:1
Turn circle	39' 9"

BRAKES
Type	Duo-Servo, single anchor hydraulic, drum type
Drum diameter	11 inches
Total swept area	259.2 square inches

CHASSIS & BODY
Frame	Ladder type, channel side rails
Body construction	All steel
Body style	Half-ton pickup

SUSPENSION
Front	I-beam axle, semi-elliptical leaf springs
Rear	Conventional; semi-elliptical leaf springs
Tires	6.50/16 6-ply (optional; 6.00/16 standard)
Wheels	Steel disc, drop-center rims

WEIGHTS AND MEASURES
Wheelbase	116 inches
Overall length	196 inches
Overall width	70 inches
Overall height	74 inches
Length of bed	78 inches
Width of bed	50 inches
Front track	58.25 inches
Rear track	60.5 inches
Ground clearance	10 inches
Gross vehicle wgt.	4,200 pounds
Shipping weight	3,240 pounds

CAPACITIES
Crankcase	5 quarts
Cooling system	15 quarts
Fuel tank	17.5 gallons

CALCULATED DATA
Horsepower/c.i.d.	.425
Pounds/hp	35.2
Pounds/c.i.d.	15.0

Right: Plenty of room for working in this engine compartment. **Facing page, top left:** Truck sits well, with lots of back and leg support. **Top right:** Tailgate is supported by simple chains. **Center left:** Outside mirror is another example of Chevy's functional approach to truck design of the time. **Center right:** Everything the driver needs to know is right in front in the two round instrument clusters. **Bottom:** Corner windows in the cab gave Chevy drivers superior visibility.

1952 CHEVROLET

range of trucks was introduced. Mechanically these vehicles were much like their predecessors, apart from their use of precision-type bearings—an improvement that seemed to many of us to be long overdue. But the styling was completely revised. More than ever, with Chevrolet, a truck was a truck. Resembling neither the passenger cars nor any previous Chevy commercial vehicle, this new model was recognizable as a Chevrolet chiefly by its bow-tie emblem.

The theme remained largely unchanged for several years. By 1954 there was a new, one-piece, curved-glass windshield that was a distinct improvement—and a revamped grille that clearly was not.

Rival Ford, meanwhile, had not been idle. Its F-1 pickup, so popular with today's collectors, made its debut shortly after the 1948 Chevrolet trucks were introduced. And for 1952 Ford replaced its flathead six with a new, overhead-valve powerplant of nearly square dimensions. The old L-head V-8 was continued in production for a couple more years before being replaced by a more modern design.

Officially, the Ford six was listed at 95 horsepower—three more than the Chevrolet, five fewer than the familiar Ford V-8. In reality, this new powerplant—the most up-to-date six-cylinder engine on the American market at that time—was almost certainly underrated, in order to preserve the theoretical advantage of the eight-cylinder unit.

One might have expected the new engine to give Ford the advantage over Chevrolet, but it didn't. Ford's share of the truck market dropped, ironically, to a post-war low in 1952.

There were still better days ahead for Chevrolet: 1955 brought a host of innovations including an optional V-8 engine and GM's HydraMatic transmission, with twelve-volt electrics standard. High-styled, "Fleetside" cabs carried

wraparound windshields, "dogleg" and all. There was even an uptown edition called the Cameo Carrier (see page 16), featuring a full-width body, Bel Air hubcaps, chromed grille and an eye-catching wraparound rear window, all done up in a Bombay Ivory finish with bright red trim. This one proved to be a trendsetter, paving the way for later generations of fashionable, gussied-up pickups. ᦏ

Acknowledgments and Bibliography

Automotive Industries *(various issues)*; Tad Burness, American Truck Spotters Guide, 1920–1970; *Chevrolet factory literature*; George H. Dammann, Sixty Years of Chevrolet; *General Motors Corporation, Chevrolet Division,* The Chevrolet Story; *G.N. Georgano (ed.),* The Complete Encyclopedia of Commercial Vehicles; The New York Times, *June 7, 1941; James K. Wagner,* Ford Trucks Since 1905; *James A. and Genevieve J. Wren,* Motor Trucks of America.

Our thanks to Irv Neubert, executive secretary, Light Commercial Vehicle Association, Jonesborough, Tennessee. Special thanks to Bob Rocchio, Newport Beach, California.

drive report

Detroit's first glamour truck, the fleet-sided Chevrolet Cameo Carrier elevated the pickup from its traditional workhorse status and made it respectable enough for suburbanites.

By Michael Lamm, *Editor*

PHOTOS BY BILL OWENS

CAMEO

THE SAME THING that happened to the postwar station wagon happened to the postwar pickup—it just took a little longer.

Both moved up off the ranch and into the suburbs. Today, the pickup enjoys a respectable, pampered life alongside the wagon in many of America's better garages.

The glamour truck got its start with the 1955 Chevrolet Cameo Carrier, just as the modern, popular, steel-bodied station wagon took hold with the 1949 Plymouth Suburban wagon.

Before the Cameo, pickups ranked as trucks: utility vehicles. They rode like trucks,

handled like trucks, steered like trucks, sounded and smelled like trucks. Pickups weren't conveyances most women cared to be seen in, much less drive.

But the Cameo changed all that. The Cameo became America's first production glamour truck, and by making the pickup palatable to (among others) housewives, we can safely say that it's at least as important in the history of American autodom as the all-steel station wagon. Today, both pickups and wagons are so widely accepted that we take them very much for granted.

The Cameo shook off its truck image in a number of clever ways. The first Cameos, like

early Corvettes, were all painted white (actually Bombay Ivory). The predominant overall impression was one of clean lines and tidiness. And the Cameo introduced that important innovation, the fleet-sided box. Add to that the bright red accents around the cab, the full wheelcovers, abundant chrome, large glass area, passenger-car-like interior, the wide range of accessories, and you had a graceful, distinctive, comfortable, respectable vehicle— a pickup no one feared being seen in.

The Cameo's option list alone took it out of the truck category: power steering and brakes, 4-speed Hydra-Matic or 4-speed synchromesh, V-8, overdrive, and electric wipers were only a few. Standard equipment, by the way, included the Chevy 6 with 3-speed column shift, but not too many buyers ordered Cameos that way. Like Nomads, Chevy's fleetsided pickups tended to get optionalized.

The man in charge of developing the Cameo was Luther W. (Lu) Stier, head of Chevrolet's truck studio from 1949 to 1962, a veteran designer/illustrator who'd worked under Ken Coppock in Chevy's car studios before WW-II. Mr. Stier was head of GM's design operations in Brazil until his recent retirement.

When we asked him to tell us the story of the Cameo's development, Lu Stier answered with the following letter:

"I am very pleased to furnish you with my recollections of the Chevrolet Cameo pickup.

"The person very much responsible for the idea was a young designer named Charles M. (Chuck) Jordan.

"Much credit for the engineering of the vehicle must be given to Mr. Edward N. (Ed) Cole, then chief engineer of Chevrolet, and Mr. E.J. (Jim) Premo, Cole's assistant.

"I remember having many lively discussions with Mr. Cole regarding my feeling that Chevrolet needed a more modern concept with respect to its existing truck line. The division became quite enthusiastic over the idea of a 'fleetsided' pickup.

"The fleetside was originally designed with an integral cab and pickup box. Engineering made prototypes for testing and found that

there was no way to counter frame torquing— that with an integral box, the sheet metal at the back of the cab tended to wrinkle.

"At that point, the division was practically ready to abandon the idea, but our studio insisted we could separate the cab and box without losing the desirable exterior appearance.

"It was about this time that the accountants determined that we couldn't really afford to make the pickup box out of steel—that the cost of the new tools and dies would be too much for the projected low production volume.

"We were then able to convince the division that we could keep the existing stepside box and simply add fiberglass panels flush with the cab sides. We also added a fiberglass cover to the existing tailgate. The result became the first Cameo Carrier of 1955.

"The basic front-end sheet metal was very much the design of young Chuck Jordan. Bob Phillips also contributed much to this program. Both men are still with GM Design at the Tech Center.

"The interior layout, gauges, upholstery, and so forth became the responsibility of Drew Hare, who was then chief designer for truck interiors. We made clay models of this project in what was then known as Fisher Body Plant 8."

Chuck Jordan, the young designer in Mr. Stier's studio, is now GM's corporate director of design, with responsibility for all

exterior and interior design studios, plus advanced, international, and industrial design. Mr. Jordan very kindly filled me in on the Cameo's nascence during a lunch in Dearborn, Michigan, last July.

He told me that he'd always been very much interested in truck styling, so much so that he'd written his graduate thesis at MIT on the topic, *Heavy-Duty Mack Truck Styling*. "I've always loved trucks," he told me. His degree from MIT, incidentally, was in mechanical engineering, not design. His natural automotive design ability was supplemented with courses at MIT's school of architecture.

Jordan entered GM in late 1949 and served his apprenticeship, as was then the custom, in experimental styling. The experimental studio happened to be in Plant 8, right down the hall from Lu Stier's truck studio, and it wasn't long before Jordan moved into trucks.

"It was a very small studio," he recounted. "We first worked on a facelift of the truck Chevy had introduced in 1948. Then, in June 1952, I got called up as a second lieutenant in the Air Force reserves, and they sent me to Patrick AFB, which is now Cape Canaveral.

"So, what sort of job do you suppose the Air Force assigned me? Well, since I had a degree in mechanical engineering from MIT, they put me in charge of the motor pool, what else?"

But, with a little finagling, Jordan got himself out of the motor pool and into a small art department on base. "They did charts and presentations for Congress," he explained, adding that he had plenty of time after hours to do

Owen Owens's 1956 Chevrolet Cameo pickup gives a choppy ride when unloaded, but its solid front axle keeps it from leaning in hard cornering.

1956 Chevrolet Cameo

drawings of what interested him most, namely trucks. And that's where the Cameo was born—at an Air Force Base art studio in Florida.

JORDAN WAS RELEASED from active duty in 1953 and returned to his job in Detroit. "It was about time to start the new truck program. We'd been anticipating the new truck with sketches that some of the other guys and I were doing in the studio. Lu had given us enough time; we weren't that busy, so we could sit and do some advanced doodling."

It was at this point that Stier got together with Cole to work out the same sort of leap in truck design as the 1955 Chevrolet represented in passenger cars. Chevy trucks hadn't gotten more than minor facelifts since 1948, while Ford had introduced the F-l for 1951 and extensively revamped it as the F-100 for 1953.

Division general manager Thomas H. Keating agreed that it was time to update all of Chevy's trucks, as did sales manager William E. Fish. Fish believed strongly in the maxim "styling sells," so Chevrolet's divisional chiefs had little trouble convincing GM's top corporate brass.

Stier responded by showing Cole Jordan's work, and Cole felt that Jordan's drawings were definitely in the right direction.

Chuck Jordan continues: "We worked late one night, because we were going to have an important product policy meeting on the new truck program the next day. We were all working hard by this time, trying to figure out how to get this sleek-sided job sold. We'd been working overtime in the truck studio to get this program going. That night we finished a 3/8-scale illustration. It was really done around the cab that we were developing for the entire truck line. It wasn't just some designer's sketch. It was actually designed as the model for this line of trucks. And that really got the thing in focus. Reception to the design was so good that we decided to model it, and once it was modeled, there wasn't any question."

The Cameo, then, became the centerpiece for Chevy's first truly new truck line in eight years.

FLEETSIDED PICKUPS weren't entirely new—Australian "utes" had had them for some time, and with integral beds at that. So did the California-built Powell Sport Wagon, a limited-production pickup of fiberglass-and-steel construction.

In its earliest proposals, the Cameo's cab and bed were to form a single unit, as Lu Stier mentioned. But Jim Premo, the Chevrolet engineer, predicted sheet-metal distortion from frame torquing, and tests soon confirmed him. So if the Cameo could be built at all, it would have to be with a non-connected bed.

"We fought and fought and fought," recalls Jordan, "and it wasn't a matter of economics

Above: Chevrolet's truck studio in 1953 saw considerable activity toward first big restyle since 1948. The 1955 trucks were to reflect the same radical changes as '55 Chevy passenger cars. Studio boss Lu Stier is in suit in background. **Below:** *Chuck Jordan began these far-out pickups while still in the Air Force in Florida. When he got back to Detroit, he showed his doodlings to Lu Stier, and that eventually led to America's first glamour truck, the 1955 Chevy Cameo.*

CHARLES M. JORDAN COLLECTION

so much as structure. We wanted to keep the clean look of an integral cab and pickup box. But there was too much twist between the cab and the box. So we had to put in some clearance—I think it was about an inch. It really hurt us to do that, but in retrospect it worked out all right."

As the design turned out, the cab ended in vertical sheet-metal flanges behind the doors. These flanges fit into the front of the pickup box, thus minimizing the severity of the gap. It was further softened by a chrome trim strip at the leading edge of the box.

The Cameo, of course, had to fit into Chevrolet's overall truck program, with as much sheet-metal interchangeability as possible. Jordan stresses that all conventional Chevy and GMC pickups and trucks of that era shared basic cabs, from the half-ton 3100 series through the 2-ton 5700s. The bigger trucks got broader fenders and stood higher off the ground, but their central cab structures were all identical.

As mentioned, the Cameo's outer pickup box was formed from fiberglass, as was the skin of the tailgate. Fabrication of these panels was handled by the same people who supplied Corvette bodies: Moulded Fiberglass of Ashtabula, Ohio.

Chevy trucks of 1955 took their styling themes, both inside and out, from the division's all-new passenger cars. The hawkish hooded headlights were borrowed from Cadillac, Ferrari inspired the eggcrate grille, and the pie-wedge instrument cluster followed the Corvette motif. This meant that Chevrolet cars and trucks all shared a common identity: They were recognizable as members of the same family.

CHEVROLET BUILT the Cameo for four model years, 1955–58, inclusive. The 1955 versions came only in white, with red around the cab and inside the box. For 1956, Cameos listed eight different colors, each with contrasting colors on the fleetside inserts and around the cab's glass areas. For 1957, Cameos became available in additional colors. Chevrolet made grille and trim changes from year to year, and in the Cameo's last year, 1958, it took on quad headlights.

Normal load capacity of the half-ton Cameo was 500 pounds, but with optional heavy-duty equipment, payload ratings could be boosted to 1,500 pounds. Since that era's Chevrolet stepside pickups had identical inner beds, cargo volume was the same.

Chevrolet lists 10,320 Cameos sold in its four years of production. This breaks down as follows:

    1955 5,219
    1956 2,154
    1957 2,572
    1958 375

The reason so few were sold in 1958 is because the Cameo had suddenly gotten stiff competition from the 1958 Apache Fleetside, which had a slab-sided, all-*metal* pickup box. It wasn't quite so luxurious as the Cameo, but it also cost less.

Mechanically, Cameos shared engines with passenger cars—the 235.5-c.i.d. Stovebolt 6

GM DESIGN STAFF

Above: Initial Cameo concept called for integrating cab and pickup box. Original grille texture and headlight brows borrowed from Chevy passenger-car styling. *Below and right:* Full-sized clay model and initial fiberglass mockup also carried through with one-piece construction. Testing soon showed that frame twisting wrinkled metal behind the cab, and designers reluctantly agreed to a one-inch gap between cab and box.

GM DESIGN STAFF

Cameo taillights seem to be adaptations of 1954 Chevrolet car lamps.

1956 Chevrolet Cameo

*Above left: Cameo's standard wheelcovers were a modification of the car's. **Above center:** Chevrolet's light trucks and its passenger cars shared the small-block V-8 during the Cameo's lifetime. This engine is still very much with us nearly a quarter century later. **Above right:** The rear tires spin freely due to lightness of rear without a load. Wraparound windshield and back glass give excellent visibility. **Below:** Cameo's interior in red and white seems posh compared to most pickups of that day. Many buyers ordered their Cameos fully optionized.*

being standard, with 265 and 283 V-8s optional. We've covered the development of these powerplants in some detail previously (see *SIA* #9 and #27), so we won't repeat here.

Chevrolet hit the Daytona NASCAR International Speed Trials pretty hard in 1956, at a time when the factory still raced out in the open. Smokey Yunick, the famous race mechanic, piloted a modified Cameo through the Daytona clocks that year to set a new Class 5 record for standing-mile acceleration: 89.524 mph. A Cameo also took the flying mile, but we have no record of its speed, driver, or modifications. *Motor Trend* briefly tested a McCulloch-blown 1956 Cameo and published a 0-60-mph time of 8.7 seconds, with the quarter mile in 17.6.

YOU SIT UP HIGH in a Cameo, with remarkable visibility in all directions. Except for a touch of distortion in the corners of the wraparound windshield (and to a lesser degree through the neatly wrapped backlight), this cab gives an absolutely panoramic view.

Owen Owens, genial proprietor of the new Ragtime auto and boat museum in Oakland-

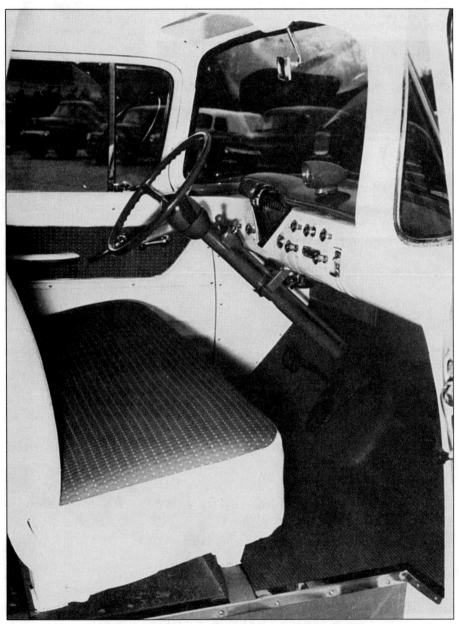

The Wraparound Windshield

THE CAMEO shared GM's dramatically wrapped windshield throughout its life (1955–58). As a styling device, the wraparound windshield no doubt contributed to the glamour and, thereby, the sales of quite a number of GM cars.

However, a controversy soon dimmed the popularity of the wraparound windshield and eventually led to its discontinuance.

It wasn't hard to see that the sharp bends in the glass made for visual distortion. Dr. DuPont Guerry of the Medical College of Virginia wrote in *Science Digest* in 1956 that wraparound windshields "violate all basic optical principles." He said they also created "ghosts," or double vision, and distorted via the prism effect.

General Motors answered in the next issue of *Science Digest*, defending the wraparound windshield as "the safest we have ever developed." GM cited tests at the Dartmouth Medical School that pronounced wraparounds better and more comfortable than conventional windshields.

Meanwhile, the public sided with Dr. Guerry and added bumped knees and high replacement costs to its list of complaints. By 1961, the romance with wraparound windshields had pretty much dimmed.

GM DESIGN STAFF

specifications

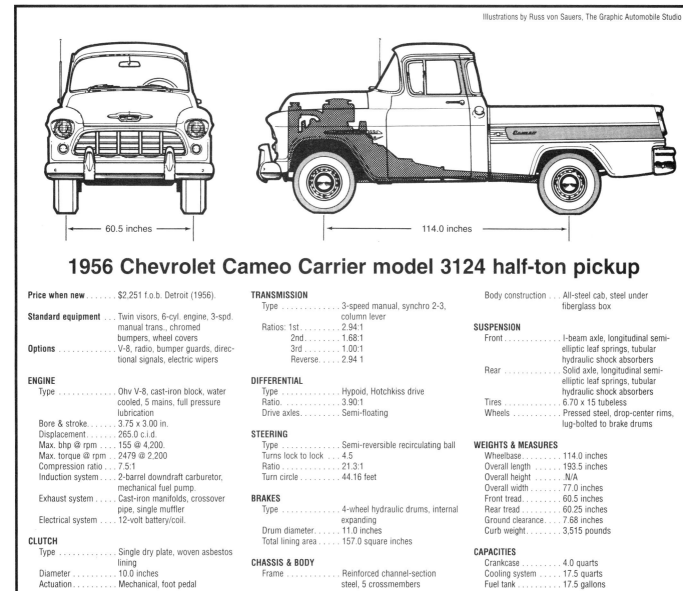

60.5 inches

114.0 inches

1956 Chevrolet Cameo Carrier model 3124 half-ton pickup

Price when new . . . . $2,251 f.o.b. Detroit (1956).

Standard equipment . . . Twin visors, 6-cyl. engine, 3-spd. manual trans., chromed bumpers, wheel covers

Options . . . . V-8, radio, bumper guards, directional signals, electric wipers

ENGINE
Type . . . . Ohv V-8, cast-iron block, water cooled, 5 mains, full pressure lubrication
Bore & stroke . . . . 3.75 x 3.00 in.
Displacement . . . . 265.0 c.i.d.
Max. bhp @ rpm . . . . 155 @ 4,200.
Max. torque @ rpm . . . 2479 @ 2,200
Compression ratio . . . 7.5:1
Induction system . . . . 2-barrel downdraft carburetor, mechanical fuel pump.
Exhaust system . . . . . Cast-iron manifolds, crossover pipe, single muffler
Electrical system . . . . 12-volt battery/coil.

CLUTCH
Type . . . . Single dry plate, woven asbestos lining
Diameter . . . . 10.0 inches
Actuation . . . . Mechanical, foot pedal

TRANSMISSION
Type . . . . 3-speed manual, synchro 2-3, column lever
Ratios: 1st 2.94:1
2nd 1.68:1
3rd 1.00:1
Reverse 2.94 1

DIFFERENTIAL
Type . . . . Hypoid, Hotchkiss drive
Ratio 3.90:1
Drive axles . . . . Semi-floating

STEERING
Type . . . . Semi-reversible recirculating ball
Turns lock to lock . . . 4.5
Ratio 21.3:1
Turn circle . . . . 44.16 feet

BRAKES
Type . . . . 4-wheel hydraulic drums, internal expanding
Drum diameter . . . . . . 11.0 inches
Total lining area . . . . 157.0 square inches

CHASSIS & BODY
Frame . . . . Reinforced channel-section steel, 5 crossmembers

Body construction . . . All-steel cab, steel under fiberglass box

SUSPENSION
Front . . . . I-beam axle, longitudinal semi-elliptic leaf springs, tubular hydraulic shock absorbers
Rear . . . . Solid axle, longitudinal semi-elliptic leaf springs, tubular hydraulic shock absorbers
Tires . . . . 6.70 x 15 tubeless
Wheels . . . . Pressed steel, drop-center rims, lug-bolted to brake drums

WEIGHTS & MEASURES
Wheelbase . . . . 114.0 inches
Overall length . . . . . 193.5 inches
Overall height . . . . . . N/A
Overall width . . . . . . 77.0 inches
Front tread . . . . 60.5 inches
Rear tread . . . . 60.25 inches
Ground clearance . . . . 7.68 inches
Curb weight . . . . 3,515 pounds

CAPACITIES
Crankcase . . . . 4.0 quarts
Cooling system . . . . . 17.5 quarts
Fuel tank . . . . 17.5 gallons

CHEVROLET MOTOR DIV.　　CHEVROLET MOTOR DIV.

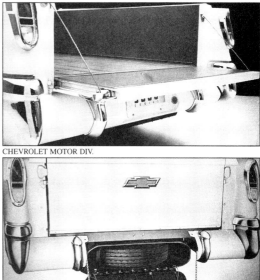

CHEVROLET MOTOR DIV.

Above left: With business going slowly on the Corvette in the mid-1950s, Moulded Fiberglas, of Ashtabula, Ohio, took on the assignment of supplying fiberglass for Cameo's pickup box, outer tailgate, and spare carrier. Above right: Clean inner surfaces of pickup box are painted red, with cables similar to Nomad's and hidden hinges and latches. Right: Spare tire lives behind the swing-down center section of the sheet-metal rear bumper.

Above: Cab extends back into pickup box via flares, barely visible here. Below: Cameo grille changed each model year, and other colors besides white and red became available with the 1956 model.

1956 Chevrolet Cameo

Emeryville, California, was kind enough to let *SIA* photograph and drive his original, 40,000-mile 1956 Cameo.

I found acceleration very strong indeed, with enough power from the 265-c.i.d. V-8 to make wheelspin a problem. I had to be careful not to break loose the tires when starting out on gravel, and the 3-speed column shifter almost invites chirping in second. There's very little weight over the rear wheels unless the pickup is carrying a load.

This rear-end lightness also affects ride. The Cameo's ride, unloaded, tends to be choppy. I suspect that 500 pounds in the bed would smooth the ride considerably.

Chevrolet still used the I-beam front axle under its 1956 trucks, including the Cameo. The solid axle does its part toward the choppy ride, but on the other hand it holds the pickup very steady in hard cornering. No need for a sway bar up front. There's little or no lean on corners, but it takes a bit of care to counter the Cameo's natural tendency to understeer; also to keep the rear end from scooting out and getting away when powering through sweepers.

One very impressive aspect of the Cameo is its quietness: no traditional creaks and groans, as in so many pickups, no tailgate chains to rattle, and not even any noticeable sloshing from the gas tank behind the seat. Apparently the cab is well insulated, and the fuel tank has plenty of internal baffles. In that way, it's like a car. Seats stand high and upright and hit a happy medium between too firm and too soft. There's just the right amount of give. Instruments, steering wheel position, and pedals are likewise comfortable and handy.

Soon after the Cameo came out, competitors began bringing out similar pickups. In May 1957, Dodge introduced the Sweptside 100: fleetsided and with fiberglass fins. That year, too, Ford launched the Ranchero which, while based on the passenger car, took its direction from the Cameo and its success as a luxury pickup.

Cameos tend to be rare today, and most of those left are still in service and don't enjoy the semi-retired status of collectors' cars. A few prime examples show up regularly at Classic Chevrolet Club and National Nomad Club meets, but so far there's no group devoted, exclusively to Cameos. Maybe it's time. ෨

Our thanks to Luther W. Stier, GM do Brasil, Sao Paulo; Charles M. Jordan, Tom Christiansen, Drew Hare, and Jim Brady, GM Design Staff, Warren, Michigan; Jim Williams, Chevrolet Public Relations, Detroit; Noland Adams, Albany, California; Gary Mortimer, Harrison, Ohio; Bob Wingate, San Dimas, California; Doug Moorhead and Skip Lile of the Classic Chevy Club, Box 17188, Orlando, Florida 32810; and Wayne Oakley, National Nomad Club, Box 606, Arvada, Colorado 80001. Special thanks to Owen Owens Ragtime Museum, 5800 Shellmound, Emeryville, California.

You won't find all these hour-saving, dollar-saving

'55 CHEVROLET TRUCK FEATURES *anywhere else!*

Dollar-Saving Engine Features

You get exactly the right power for your job. All three great valve-in-head engines deliver gas-saving, hour-saving high-compression performance. Aluminum alloy pistons, all-weather ignition system, full-pressure lubrication, assure long low-cost life!

Trip-Saving Body Features

Chevrolet-built, Unit-Designed truck bodies last longer, require less maintenance. What's more, you haul big loads, save time and extra trips. New stake and platform bodies are wide, long and roomy. Spacious pickups have sturdy tailgates that close grain-tight!

Long-Life Chassis Features

Sturdy single-unit tubular steel rear axle housings! Strong and rigid frames! Durable Diaphragm Spring Clutches with high torque capacities and long-life construction. Spring capacity is matched to tire capacity for dependable performance.

Advance-Design Cab Features

Assured driver comfort with efficient ventilation and insulation; shackle mountings that cushion frame vibrations; a one-piece curved windshield with full-width defroster outlet. The all-steel Double-Wall cab construction means extra safety and durability.

Work-Saving Control Features

Less effort needed with Recirculating-Ball Steering Gear; Torque-Action and Twin-Action brake design helps you stop more surely and easily. Proved truck Hydra-Matic Transmission, optional on ½-, ¾- and 1-ton models at extra cost, eliminates clutching and gearshifting.

Take a good look at these '55 Chevrolet truck features, if you will. See how they'll save hours and dollars and driving effort on your hauling job. Then consider this: You won't find all these worthwhile advances in any other truck at any price. It's a fact! Chevrolet trucks bring you the features you want for '55 . . . the savings you want for years to come! See your Chevrolet dealer. . . . Chevrolet Division of General Motors, Detroit 2, Michigan

CHEVROLET ADVANCE-DESIGN TRUCKS

PERT PICKUP

1946 DODGE SERIES WC

J UST about everybody knows that, with the coming of World War II, passenger car production was halted by government fiat on February 1, 1942. Often overlooked, however, is the fact that the manufacture of civilian trucks followed suit just a few weeks later.

At Dodge, for instance, production of commercial vehicles was halted on April 30, 1942, in order that the factory could concentrate upon the production of military trucks. Not that products of this nature were unfamiliar to Dodge. Over the previous two years the division had been building, in limited numbers, half-ton 4x4 vehicles for the United States Army. Several configurations were supplied, command reconnaissance cars and weapons carriers being the most

By Arch Brown
Photos by Bud Juneau

numerous. A total of 4,641 of these machines were built for the government in 1940, which amounted to only about four percent of Dodge's total truck output for the year. But the 4x4s gave an excellent account of themselves, and as world tensions increased, so did Dodge's military orders.

For that matter, military production was not a novel experience for Dodge, even in 1940. As early as 1916—barely two years after John and Horace Dodge commenced passenger car production —General Pershing praised the perfor-

mance of the Dodge Brothers vehicles that had taken part in his Mexican expedition against Pancho Villa. And Dodge Brothers ambulances, troop carriers and utility trucks played an important role with the American Expeditionary Force during the First World War.

Dodge trucks destined for the army numbered 79,307 during 1941. Additional types were supplied, including more than 6,000 ambulances. Most of these units, incidentally, were powered by the 217.8-cubic-inch engine first employed by Dodge in its 1934 passenger cars, though the 230.2-c.i.d. flat-head six was employed for some types starting in October 1941.

Three-quarter ton 4x4s, lower, wider and stouter than the earlier half-ton types, were introduced during April

Driving Impressions

Ed Barwick, Chrysler-Dodge-Plymouth dealer for Napa, California, and a veteran Mopar collector, bought our driveReport pickup early in 1989 from the son of the man who had driven it from Day One. Unfortunately, Ed neglected to make a note of the man's name, which became lost in the process of transferring the truck's out-of-state title. But here's the biography of our little pickup as it was recounted to us by Ed:

The Blue Flame Gas Company of Salem, Oregon, had been among the firms that had long awaited the delivery of a new pickup truck. They were one of the lucky ones, for included in the first postwar shipment of Dodge trucks to reach the Portland area was a half-ton pickup, painted in bright Dodge Truck Orange and destined for the Blue Flame Gas Company.

The truck was assigned to one of the firm's employees, and for the next 27 years this man used the pickup in the course of his daily work. He must have developed a good deal of respect (and even affection) for the little half-tonner because, upon his retirement, he arranged to buy it from his employers.

The story excited our curiosity and we made some long-distance telephone calls to see what we could learn about the Blue Flame Gas Company and the man who had driven the Dodge for so many years. We were told that, yes, there had been a Blue Flame Gas Company in Salem not so many years ago, but that it is no longer listed with Directory Assistance. So our quest came to an abrupt close.

But to return to the story, as Ed Barwick heard it from our mystery man's son: As the years went along, this man undertook to restore the Dodge. Exactly what was done by way of mechanical renovation, we do not know. But, at some point, rather extensive work must have been undertaken, for although wear on the steel pedals betrays many miles of use, the pickup is in excellent condition in every respect.

In time the truck was given a careful cosmetic restoration, including new upholstery and a sparkling finish in the original orange and black color scheme. A black vinyl tonneau cover adds a smart finishing touch, and there were further embellishments: Fenders, grille and front bumper had been decoratively striped. A nice job, Ed reports, but not strictly authentic. Barwick is a stickler for authenticity in his collector vehicles, so of course the black portions were repainted at his shop.

Upon the death of the pickup's owner, his son had used it for a time, Ed was told, though it remained the property of the owner's widow. And then she relocated to St. Helena, California. Ed Barwick, in nearby Napa, heard about the truck and after some negotiation was able to add it to his collection.

Taking the pickup for a short drive, we were pleasantly surprised at how easily it handles. The seat is fixed in one position, which often creates a serious problem for the tall driver. In this case, though another inch or so of leg room would have been welcome, we had no problem settling in behind the wheel. Admittedly, the backrest is too vertical for comfort, but who ever said a truck was supposed to be comfortable? Not in 1946, anyway.

The engine starts quickly and easily, sounding very familiar to one who owned six-cylinder Plymouths in years gone by. Clutch action is smooth, and the floor-mounted gearshift is easy to use. This is a three-speed transmission, synchronized on second and top gears, so of course it shifts like a passenger car.

There's no independent suspension here. Nobody was providing that sort of decadence in a pickup truck, back in 1946. So, naturally, there is some choppiness in the ride. It isn't bad, however. For a commercial vehicle of its generation, this one is really relatively smooth. Steering is lighter than we had expected, though a power assist would be welcome when it comes to parallel parking. And the Dodge maintains its equilibrium well in hard cornering.

Acceleration is brisk—again, by 1946 standards—and the noise level is not excessive as long as the truck is held to moderate speeds. There isn't any sound insulation to speak of, so of course, at freeway speeds the engine sounds busy.

It would be interesting to compare the half-ton Dodge pickup with its competitors, not only from Chevrolet and Ford but also from International Harvester and Studebaker. Statistically, the Dodge stacks up very well (see comparison table, page 29). Only the Ford V-8 has a larger engine and, apart from the Ford, none of the others can match the Dodge's 95 horsepower. The Dodge's wheelbase is the longest in the group, its compression ratio the highest, and it is heavier by more than a hundred pounds than its nearest competitor. Prices, of course, were set by the Office of Price Administration and were subject to change from time to time. But, in general, Dodge was able to maintain a competitive position in that respect.

The buyer had little opportunity to exercise his preference in 1946. He was lucky to get a new pickup at all, and he could count himself extremely fortunate if he was able to purchase the truck of his choice. But if, somehow, he *was* able to choose, in view of its many desirable features and its long-standing reputation for toughness and dependability, it seems to us that the Dodge would have been an excellent selection.

Left: *Grille is utilitarian.* **Above:** *But Dodge badge is highlighted in chrome.* **Below left:** *Sidelamps hang off cowl. Ram hood ornament is somewhat abstract.*

1946 DODGE

1942. By 1943 there were, in addition, 1½-ton 6x6 cargo trucks—basically weapons carriers to which a two-speed transfer case and a second differential had been added.

Civilian truck production was resumed in 1944, but on an extremely limited scale. Fewer than 8,000 such vehicles were built that year, which came to only about five percent of Dodge's truck production during 1941. That number was increased to 28,405 in 1945, still hardly enough to make a

dent in the pent-up demand. By that time large numbers of pre-war trucks in commercial use were ready for the scrap heap, and the need for replacements was becoming critical.

Vehicles supplied to the army, even the command reconnaissance cars which were essentially military passenger vehicles, were brutal to drive, as this writer can personally attest. Significantly more so, for instance, than the 1½-ton 4x4 trucks being supplied to the armed forces by Chevrolet. The Dodge's four-speed spur-gear transmission was tricky to shift without clashing. The steering was very heavy, as was brake pedal pressure. But the Dodge military trucks proved to be all but indestructi-

ble. And indeed, the 4x4s went on to serve in the Korean War, and remained in production in the guise of civilian Power Wagons, as late as 1968.

By war's end, Dodge had supplied some 400,000 trucks to the U.S. military. But with the surrender of Japan, a number of uncompleted contracts were cancelled and the reconversion to peacetime production began. Dodge's 1946 line of civilian trucks was announced in December 1945. Customers were literally standing in line awaiting their chance to buy, at long last, the new trucks they needed so badly.

There was no time to develop new models for the post-war market. Nor for that matter was there a need for anything different than the pre-war trucks. Given the tremendous demand for new vehicles at that time, Dodge, like its various competitors, would have been foolish to invest money in developing a new line. So it is hardly surprising that the 1946 Dodge trucks were virtually identical to the 1942 models.

For that matter, in many respects the company's light trucks strongly resembled their counterparts as far back as 1933. Take the engine: For some years Dodge had powered its light trucks with four-bangers from sister division Plymouth. But late in 1932 Plymouth replaced its four with the six-cylinder PC Series, and a few months later there appeared a new line of Dodge light trucks using the Plymouth PC engine. A 189.8-c.i.d. flathead, the "new" mill had actu-

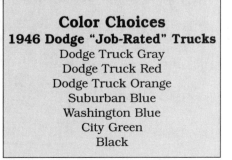

Color Choices
1946 Dodge "Job-Rated" Trucks
Dodge Truck Gray
Dodge Truck Red
Dodge Truck Orange
Suburban Blue
Washington Blue
City Green
Black

ally originated with the Dodge Division, where it had been used in the DD series of 1930–32, though certain refinements such as a higher compression ratio and downdraft carburetion had increased its output for the 1933 applications from 60 to 70 horsepower.

New styling, patterned after Dodge's passenger cars, had also been adopted for the 1933 light trucks, making them among the smartest-looking vehicles in their field. And the price, $440 for the half-ton pickup, was just ten dollars higher than the comparable Chevrolet.

The 1933 styling theme continued unchanged through 1935, though the appearance of Dodge's passenger cars was altered substantially in 1934 and revised again the following year. Then, in 1936, the Dodge light trucks were fully restyled once more, again taking their cue from the division's passenger car line. At that time, too, the wheelbase of the commercial units was stretched from 111¼ to 116 inches.

Plymouth, meanwhile, had introduced a more powerful engine for 1934. Displacing 201.3 cubic inches, it was rated

As in pre-war Dodge trucks, wipers hang from top of windshield frame.

at 77 horsepower. Detuned slightly to 75 horsepower, that same flathead six was also fitted to the Dodge half-ton trucks that year. And then for 1935 it was further detuned, as fitted to the commercial vehicles, to 70 horsepower. An entirely different engine was used by

Dodge for its 1937–38 light trucks. A longer block than the previous unit, it shared the 3⅜-inch bore of the Chrysler and De Soto sixes, but at 4⅜ inches its stroke was shorter by ⁷⁄₁₆ of an inch. It was rated at 75 horsepower.

Not since 1933 had Dodge light trucks

The Clone: Plymouth Pickup, 1937–1941

Ever since the early 1930s, the Chrysler Corporation had used "dual" dealerships in which Chrysler, De Soto and Dodge agencies also handled the low-priced Plymouth. The practice doubtless kept many dealers alive during the Depression, and it provided Plymouth, a relative newcomer in 1931 (when this practice began), with an exceptionally large sales network. Almost unquestionably the arrangement outlived its usefulness, for it was permitted to continue through the late 1950s, but that's not our concern here.

From the perspective of De Soto and Chrysler dealers, however, the situation was not entirely equitable. As late as 1940, Dodge consistently outsold Chrysler and De Soto put together, usually by a wide margin. Consider the numbers:

	Dodge	De Soto	Chrysler	Combined
1933	91,403	20,186	30,220	50,406
1934	108,687	15,825	36,929	52,754
1935	211,752	34,276	50,010	84,286
1936	274,904	52,789	71,295	124,084
1937	288,841	86,541	107,872	194,413
1938	106,370	32,688	41,496	74,184
1939	186,474	53,269	67,749	121,018
1940	225,595	83,805	115,824	199,629

Then, to make matters worse, the Dodge dealers had the further advantage of Dodge Division's truck line with which to supplement their passenger-car volume.

A few Plymouth "Commercial Sedans" were manufactured during 1930–31, but these were nothing more than modified two-door passenger cars, and, in any case, only 80 were built. A similar body type followed, in 1935–36, this time in somewhat less limited numbers. Commencing in 1934, some Plymouth chassis were fitted with station-wagon bodies manufactured by the U.S. Body and Forging Company of Tell City, Indiana. Oddly enough, it wasn't until 1940 that Plymouth considered the station wagon to be a passenger car, rather than a part of the division's commercial line.

From the dealers' perspective—that is, the Chrysler/Plymouth and De Soto/Plymouth dealers—it wasn't enough. They wanted light trucks. No reason why not, from a manufacturing standpoint. Chrysler Corporation had always shared components throughout the several passenger-car lines, so why not do the same with the trucks?

The result was the first Plymouth pickup, introduced as part of the 1937 commercial line. And, sure enough, in most respects it was a clone of the half-ton Dodge. We said "in most respects";

there were two principal differences. The first was the front-end styling. Grille and hood had clearly been inspired by the 1936 Plymouth passenger cars. And under that hood was Plymouth's 201.3-c.i.d. flathead six, detuned from 82 to 70 horsepower. Dodge's light trucks, meanwhile, were powered by a 218.1-cubic-inch, 75-horsepower mill. At $525 f.o.b. factory, the Plymouth was priced $15.00 below the Dodge, $10.00 higher than the comparable Chevrolet.

For 1939, the Plymouth pickup, like its Dodge near-twin, was completely restyled. Gone was any resemblance to the passenger-car line. The pickup now had the brawny look of a truck, which may have been useful in promoting a "rugged" image, though it did nothing for the vehicle's looks. By this time, both the Plymouth and Dodge units were fitted with the smaller engine, still rated at 70 bhp.

The chief visible change for 1940 lay in the use of sealed-beam headlamps, which necessitated placing the parking lamps in small pods fitted to the tops of the headlamp shells. Three horizontal strips of bright metal were added to the grille, presumably in order to suggest the smart new frontal appearance of that year's Plymouth passenger cars. Otherwise, it was more of the same as far as appearance was concerned. Performance was another matter, however, for although the displacement remained at 201.3 cubic inches, horsepower was raised to 79—a difference of nearly 13 percent.

1941 proved to be the final year for Plymouth's pickup. No explanation was ever offered by the Chrysler Corporation for eliminating it from the line, though the 1942 model year proved to be of such short duration that it didn't matter very much, in any case. Sales of the pickup had never been spectacular but, as the following table shows, they were fairly steady and substantial enough, presumably, to be profitable:

1937	10,709
1938	4,620
1939	6,181
1940	6,879
1941	6,073

Some sources have suggested that Chrysler, busy by then with military orders for the United States Government, needed the production capacity for the manufacture of command cars, ambulances and weapons carriers. A good line of reasoning as far as it goes, but it fails to explain why the Plymouth pickup didn't return after World War II. Surely, by the early 1950s, the dealers—especially those with the De Soto franchise—needed any help they could get.

illustrations by Russell von Sauers, The Graphic Automobile Studio

© copyright 1990, Special Interest Autos

specifications

116 inches

56.5 inches

1946 Dodge Series WC Pickup

Original price	$861 f.o.b. factory with standard equipment
Options on dR car	Deluxe cab equipment ($26.65), passenger-side windshield wiper ($4.10), heater (price not determined)
Aftermarket equip.	Dual outside mirrors, tonneau cover

ENGINE

Type	6-cylinder in-line, cast en bloc
Bore x stroke	3.25 inches x 4.75 inches
Displacement	217.76 cubic inches
Compression ratio	6.8:1
Hp @ rpm	95 @ 3,600
Torque @ rpm	172 @ 1,200–1,900
Taxable hp	25.34
Valves	L-head
Valve lifters	Mechanical
Main bearings	4
Lubrication system	Pressure
Fuel system	Stromberg BXV-3 single downdraft carburetor, mechanical pump
Cooling system	Centrifugal pump; full-length water jackets
Exhaust system	Single
Electrical system	6-volt

CLUTCH

Type	Single dry plate
Diameter	10 inches
Actuation	Mechanical, foot pedal

TRANSMISSION

Type	3-speed selective, synchronized 2nd and 3rd gears, floor-mounted lever
Ratios: 1st	2.57:1
2nd	1.83:1
3rd	1.00:1
Reverse	3.48:1

DIFFERENTIAL

Type	Hypoid
Ratio	4.10:1
Drive axles	Semi-floating

STEERING

Turns, lock to lock	4
Ratio	17:1
Turning circle	34 feet 9 inches

BRAKES

Type	4-wheel hydraulic drum type
Drum diameter	10 inches
Lining area	148.4 square inches

BODY & CHASSIS

Construction	Body-on-frame
Frame	Channel iron with 5 cross members
Body	All steel
Body style	Half-ton pickup truck

SUSPENSION

Type	Semi-elliptic springs, front and rear

Shock absorbers	Airplane type
Wheels	Steel disc
Tires	6.00/164-ply (original equipment; now 6.50/16 6 ply)

CAPACITIES

Crankcase	5 quarts
Cooling system	3.875 gallons
Fuel tank	18 gallons

WEIGHTS AND MEASURES

Wheelbase	116 inches
Overall length	191.375 inches
Overall width	71 inches
Overall height	74 inches
Front track	56.5 inches
Rear track	60 inches
Road clearance	9 inches
Weight	2,975 pounds

BED DIMENSIONS

Length	78.125 inches
Width	48.25 inches
Depth	17 inches

CALCULATED DATA

Hp per c.i.d.	.436
Weight per hp	31.3 pounds
Weight per c.i.d.	13.7 pounds
Lb. per sq. in. (brakes)	20.0 pounds

Spare hangs out under pickup bed; a typical location for trucks of the time, which made changing tires a particularly messy business.

1946 DODGE

Above left: Tailgate has unmistakable identification. **Above and below:** *Rectangular box will haul a generous amount of goods.*

shown changes as great as those represented by the 1939 model. Engine displacement reverted to 201.3 cubic inches, and horsepower was once again advertised at 70. Wheelbase remained at 116 inches, and the weight was increased by 275 pounds, which suggests that performance must have suffered somewhat, though it remained fully competitive. Torque was down just slightly, from 155 to 148 foot-pounds.

But the biggest change in Dodge's 1939 truck line had to do with styling. No longer was there any apparent effort to resemble the passenger cars; these vehicles were trucks. And they looked like trucks—sturdy, tough, functional. Nobody could have accused them of being beautiful, yet they were not unattractive. The price was cut by $10.00, to $590. Meanwhile, Chevrolet had shaved its ticket to $572, maintaining its traditional competitive edge.

Dodge called its 1939 line "the truck of the year," and took the occasion to open what was then the world's largest exclusive truck plant in Warren, Michigan. Truck production came to 89,364 for the year, including 5,704 units built in Canada, an increase of nearly 43 percent over the recession-plagued 1938 figure.

The most visible change for 1940 was the use of sealed beam headlamps,

which necessitated relocating the parking lamps to small pods mounted atop the headlamp shells. More significant were modifications to the engine, which increased the horsepower from 70 to 79, while torque was boosted from 148 to 154 foot-pounds.

Nor were changes particularly apparent in the 1941 models, though the headlamps were moved outboard, giving

Comparison Table: 1946 Half-Ton Pickups

	Dodge	Chevrolet	Ford	International	Studebaker
Price, f.o.b. factory	$861	$757	$918	$883*	$929
Wheelbase	116 inches	115 inches	114 inches	113 inches	113 inches
Weight (lbs.)	2,975	2,870	2,865	2,645*	2,710
Cylinders	6	6	V-8	6	6
Engine c.i.d.	217.8	216.5	225.8	213.3	169.6
Horsepower @ rpm	95/3,600	90/3,300	100/3,800	82/3,400	80/4,000
Compression ratio	6.8:1	6.5:1	6.75:1	6.3:1	6.5:1
Valve configuration	L-head	ohv	L-head	L-head	L-head
Tire size	6.00/16	6.00/16	6.00/1.6	6.00/16	6.50/16
* chassis and cab					

1946 DODGE

the trucks something of a bug-eyed look. Parking lamps, meanwhile, were moved to the cowl. Two-tone color schemes were available at no additional charge, an oil bath air cleaner became standard equipment, and a new high-lift camshaft increased the horsepower to 82.5 and the torque to 160.

With the introduction of the 1942 models on July 25, 1941, Plymouths were fitted with the 217.8-cubic-inch engine that had formerly powered the Dodge passenger cars, while the Dodges received a 230.2-c.i.d. block that was, in effect, a stroked version of the previous mill. Light trucks from the Dodge Division, as well as Plymouth's passenger cars, received the 217.8 unit, raising their horsepower to 95 and their torque to 172, a substantial difference and an important one in the face of competitive pressures. Frames were strengthened by means of increased stock thickness, clutch housings were beefed up, and a redesigned radiator core provided improved cooling. Visually, however, the trucks were unchanged except that bumpers, in accordance with wartime restrictions, were painted gray or black in lieu of the previous aluminum finish.

When the post-war models were at last introduced, in December 1945, no change had been made to the appearance of Dodge's light trucks. But there were a couple of unseen improvements:

Top: *Profile is businesslike rather than beautiful.* **Center:** *Interior is as straightforward as rest of truck.* **Bottom:** *Dash carries full instrumentation.*

Below: Hood opens with exterior levers, has i.d. on both sides. Right: Venerable L-head six's design goes back to early '30s.

must have been awaited by its original buyer. ᕁ

Acknowledgments and Bibliography

Automotive Industries *(various issues):* Dodge Division factory literature; Georgano, G.N. *(ed.),* Complete Encyclopedia of Commercial Vehicles; Gunnell, John *(ed.),* Standard Catalog of American Light Duty Trucks; McPherson, Thomas A., The Dodge Story; Wren, James A. and Genevieve J., Motor Trucks of America.

Our thanks to Ron Love, Portland, Oregon. Special thanks to Ed Barwick, Napa, California.

The steering gear was strengthened and its ratio increased; more comfortable seating was supplied. But, basically, it was the same rugged, businesslike truck as its pre-war counterpart.

In the half-ton line that is the focus of our attention for this driveReport, five configurations were available: chassis and cowl, chassis and cab, canopy, panel, and the pickup represented here by our featured truck. Prices were substantially higher at introduction time than those of the 1942 models and additional hikes followed as post-war inflation took its toll. The pickup, for instance, started the 1946 model year with a factory-delivered tab of $861, compared to $651 for the 1942 model. Within a year that figure would rise to $989, and by 1948 a restyled pickup, still powered by the 95-horsepower flathead six, would sell for $1,263. Given the nature of the market in those early post-war times, the cost would have been a good deal higher yet, had it not been for government price controls. In these circumstances, the reader can readily imagine the anticipation with which delivery of our featured pickup

Prices and Weights, 1946 Dodge Light Trucks

	Price	Weight
Series WC: Half-ton, 116" w/b, 217.76 c.i.d.		
Chassis and cowl	$ 682	2,375 lb.
Chassis and cab	$ 813	2,775 lb.
Pickup (6½ ft.)	$ 861	2,975 lb.
Canopy	$1,008	3,000 lb.
Panel	$ 995	3,175 lb.
Series WD-15: 3/4-ton, 120" w/b, 217.76 c.i.d.		
Chassis and cowl	$ 768	2,525 lb.
Chassis and cab	$ 900	2,925 lb.
Pickup (7½ ft.)	$ 954	3,225 lb.
Platform (7½ ft.)	$ 973	3,325 lb.
Stake (7½ ft.)	$1,012	3,550 lb.
Series WD-20: One-ton, 120" w/b, 230.2 c.i.d.		
Chassis and cowl	$ 849	2,825 lb.
Chassis and cab	$ 981	3,250 lb.
Pickup (7½ ft.)	$1,036	3,600 lb.
Platform (7½ ft.)	$1,053	3,625 lb.
Stake (7½ ft.)	$1,093	3,850 lb.
Series WD-21: One-ton, 133" w/b, 230.2 c.i.d.		
Chassis and cowl	$ 877	2,850 lb.
Chassis and cab	$1,008	3,275 lb.
Pickup (9½ ft.)	$1,076	3,675 lb.
Platform (9½ ft.)	$1,091	3,750 lb.
Stake (9½ ft.)	$1,123	4,025 lb.
Canopy	$1,203	3,400 lb.
Panel	$1,197	3,850 lb.
Series WDX: One-ton Power Wagon, 126" w/b, 230.2 c.i.d.		
Chassis and cab	$1,555	4,475 lb.
Pickup	$1,627	4,900 lb.
*(Prices shown are f.o.b. factory, with standard equipment)		

1947 Dodge Power Wagon

by John F. Katz
photos by Vince Wright

Driving Impressions

OUR appropriately Forest Green 1947 Power Wagon was purchased new by the Pennsylvania forestry service, who used it hard maintaining lookout towers and fire roads. A garage south of Carlisle bought it at a state auction around 1962, used it for miscellaneous work until the late seventies, and then sold it to a man who wanted it for hauling firewood. He soon realized that the truck was in worse shape than he suspected, so in 1985 he sold it to Bill Garland, who specializes in restoring Power Wagons and related military vehicles.

"All the seals and bearings had to be replaced," Bill told us. "It had worked all its life, and they were pretty hard miles." The bed was too far gone to be saved, but Bill found a better one abandoned in the woods near Binghamton, New York. He restored the truck to its as-delivered condition, deviating from stock specs only by installing modern locking hubs on the front wheels.

Standing on the forest floor next to one, a Power Wagon looks mighty big. But once inside, the cockpit fits snug, and the non-adjustable seat is bolted to the floor just a little closer to the wheels and pedals than I'd like. The seat itself is firm and flat and probably comfortable enough for as far and as fast as you'd want to go in a Power Wagon. With Bill riding shotgun, there's scant room between us for another passenger, and there'd be no room for that person's feet anyway, with so many levers sprouting from the floor. The gas pedal is offset to the center, so you have to lift your foot up onto the transmission hump to step on it—an odd thing to have to remember every time you move from the brake to the gas.

One advantage of a tight cockpit is that nothing is too far away, and indeed most of the Power Wagon's accessory controls are easily reached and recognized. Only the floor-mounted levers for the parking brake, transfer case, and winch demand an awkward stretch.

The clutch—and indeed, all the major controls—require surprisingly little effort. Bill recommended second gear for a level start, shifting into third at 10 mph and into high at 25. The Power Wagon launches smoothly, albeit with a cacophony of exhaust rumble, gear whine, and general mechanical clatter.

The unsynchronized gearbox shifts smooth and slick (once I've mastered its rhythm), and runs a little quieter in high.

The speedometer reads up to 80 mph, so it's pretty certain that the guy in charge of instruments had a twisted sense of humor. Bill has never pushed his truck over 45, and now I see why: The Power Wagon steers easily, but wanders aimlessly, and even at 30 mph it demands constant attention just to keep it in its lane. "The vehicle can wander quite a lot before the steering catches up to it," Bill noted. Amen. And the uncertain steering also limits confident cornering to about 25 mph.

Part of the problem, no doubt, is the Power Wagon's unbranded military-spec tires. Their tread pattern is designed for clawing through mud; on dry pavement they ride high on their central rib, minimizing the contact patch. Bill said they're worse still in rain or light snow.

Fortunately, the brakes work well—on an empty truck at any speed we dared to drive. They do require some effort, but probably no more than in a passenger car of the same vintage. The ride is hard, but not as brutal as in some modern sports cars.

Bill recommended a flying start at the long hill back to his garage. About halfway up, the truck began to lose speed, and as we dropped down to 25 mph, Bill advised me to shift down to third. The engine screamed as if it were about to grenade, and the gears howled like evil spirits in the night. I shouted my concern to Bill, but he shouted back that the engine is governed at 3,200 rpm, so it won't break, no matter how

bad it sounds. So with faith in the governor and the basic goodness of the universe, I kept my foot pressed flat to the floor. And, despite the skull-splitting racket, the truck steadily clawed back up that hill, its speedo needle stuck unwaveringly on 25 mph—and with the same gritty determination that had served its military forebears so well.

History and Background

The production of military vehicles slackened in the final years of World War II, and by the time the Japanese government surrendered on September 2, 1945, most American manufacturers were anxious to sheathe their swords and pull their plowshare tooling out of mothballs. Few of the Army's austere and specialized trucks would adapt to the civilian market. The best known

Hail the Conquering Hero

Dodge Power Wagon

exception, of course, was the Jeep, which surely saved Willys from near-instant oblivion. But there was another vehicle born and developed in the shadow of war that returned home to a long and successful life in the fields and forests and industries. It was the Dodge Power Wagon.

The Power Wagon's earliest military ancestor (or at least the first truck to look something like it) was the 1941 Dodge WC 1/2-ton—essentially a commercial truck with four-wheel drive and simplified front-end sheet metal (see "Uncle Sam's Dodges," page 55). Dodge sold 80,000 of them to both the US and the UK through early 1942. But as the war in Europe and Asia threatened to engulf the United States, our military brass worried about the limitations of this tall and tippy civilian. They wanted a lower center of gravity, better maneuverability, more room for troops and cargo, and better traction in mud and sand. Late in 1941, Dodge answered their concerns with the similarly named but completely re-engineered WC 3/4-ton—known to Dodge insiders by its project code, T214. The T214 featured a lower, wider body hugging a new double-drop frame; and new nine-inch wide "high flotation" tires with a curving tread pattern for better traction on loose surfaces. Dodge engineers widened the front tread width to the same 64.75 inches as the rear, so that the rear wheels could follow the trail already blazed by the front ones. And while

Above: The name says it all. **Below left:** *Staggered-tread tires look authentic but raise hob with direction stability on pavement.* **Bottom left:** *Taillamp design goes back to thirties.* **Bottom:** *Headlamps are somewhat vulnerable to hard knocks.* **Facing page, top:** *With its no-nonsense appearance, Power Wagon was the Hummer of its day.* **Below right:** *No mistaking what you're following.* **Bottom:** *Off-the-shelf truck-type directions are on civilian models.*

wheelbases for the half-ton had ranged from 116-122 inches, the three-quarter-ton model came in 121, 114, and even 98-inch versions for tight maneuverability.

Power was still provided by the same flathead six used in Dodge passenger cars, but that engine had grown from 218 to 230 cubic inches for 1942, and so the T214 enjoyed the same increase in displacement. Compared to the WC half-ton, horsepower swelled from 78 at 3,000 rpm to 92 at 3,200. Key mechanical parts, including the brakes and the transfer case, were strengthened. At the same time, however, Dodge cleverly en-

gineered many of the new pieces to fit the old truck, greatly simplifying parts inventories in the field. In fact, a full 80 percent of all T214 replacement parts would fit the WC half-tons already in service.

Prophetically, the November '42 issue of *Popular Science* showcased the T214 in an article titled "The Jeep Gets a Big Brother." The magazine credited the design of the new truck to the engineers of the Quartermaster Corps at the Army's Motor Transport Base in Holabird, Maryland, near Baltimore. But according to Roger Gaskill, a Dodge engineer who worked on the civilian Power

Wagon, the T214 owed its success to Belgian-born development engineer "Frenchy" Raes. Physically small, but intimidatingly tough, Raes stubbornly over-engineered the T214 for maximum ruggedness. When Chrysler bean-counters tried to substitute standard commercial parts, Raes "stood his ground" and found ways to test the civilian pieces that would guarantee their failure. "One way or the other he'd fail it," said Gaskill, "and he got his way."

After the war, surplus military trucks of all sizes were sought out by farmers, miners, and construction companies. As common as four-wheel-drive is today, it was still a novelty then for a civilian vehicle. The Jeep had it, but the Jeep was a very small truck. Dodge knew that the conservatively rated T214 could haul a 2,000-pound payload *off-road*. There would be nothing else like it on the market.

Discharging the T214 into civilian life

proved relatively simple. Dodge engineers stretched its chassis out to 126 inches, and fitted it with the same cab used on all 1939-47 Dodge commercial trucks. They kept the T214's military-style open fenders and simple welded-bar grille, but they did raise its sloping hood line for a rounder, more powerful look. (Some sources attribute the civilian version's more blunted front-end styling to a larger Dodge military truck, the 3-ton T234 or "Burma Road Truck,"

Operating the Accessories

Four-wheel drive has traveled a long, muddy road from the Power Wagon to today's high-tech, fully automatic and shift-on-the-fly systems. The Power Wagon's cab floor sprouts a veritable forest of levers to control its four-wheel-drive and accessory functions.

Furthest from the driver, all the way to the right, are the two levers for the transfer case, set one behind the other. The rear one, closer to the seat, engages the front axle when pulled back and disengages it when pushed forward. According to the owner's manual, it is not necessary to de-clutch when shifting in or out of four-wheel mode, and in fact the lever will move most easily if the driver revs the engine while the truck is rolling slightly. But Bill told us that the lever moves just as easily when the truck is standing still, and he prefers to do it that way.

The forward transfer case lever pushes forward for high and pulls back for low, so that it cannot be shifted into low unless the lever behind it is pulled back into four-wheel-drive. To move this one, the truck must be standing absolutely still while the driver double-clutches. Between low and high is a neutral position.

To use the winch, the driver must first shift the transmission into neutral. (The

manual recommends shifting the transfer case into neutral as well, but Bill told us that this isn't necessary.) The winch has its own separate clutch, operated by another lever at the front of the truck. Pushing this lever back disengages the winch, so that the cable can be pulled out manually and rigged to whatever needs winching. Then the driver pulls the winch clutch forward, climbs back into the cab and, using the main clutch, shifts the PTO lever (the flat one closest to the driver's left leg) forward to wind in the cable. Pulling the same lever all the way back lets the cable out at a controlled rate, and again there is a neutral position between the two. It is possible to engage both the winch and the axles at the same time, a useful configuration for climbing out of mud holes.

Engaging the winch lever inside the cab with the winch clutch disengaged would operate the rear PTO, if Bill's truck had one.

Dodge rated the winch at 7,500 pounds and installed an 8,000-pound shear pin. Bill said he's seen Power Wagon owners replace the shear pin with a grade-eight bolt—a big mistake, as the winch is strong enough to break even a Power Wagon's frame.

specifications

illustrations by Russell von Sauers, The Graphic Automobile Studio

64.8 inches

126.0 inches

1947 Dodge WDX Power Wagon

Base price $1,764

Std. equip. includes Front shock absorbers, oil bath air cleaner, front bumper, adjustable engine governor, dual vacuum windshield wipers, left-side sun visor

Options on dR car Deluxe cab equipment (electric wipers, dual sun visors, dome light, vent windows, left-side arm rest), heater, PTO with winch

Est. price as equipped $2,100

ENGINE
Type	6 in line
Bore x stroke	3.25 inches x4.625 inches
Displacement	2303.2 cubic inches
Compression ratio	6.7:1
Horsepower @ rpm	94 @ 3,200
Torque @ rpm	185 @ 1,200 (gross)
Taxable horsepower	25.4
Valve gear	L-head
Valve lifters	Hydraulic
Main bearings	4
Induction system	1 Stromberg downdraft with governor
Fuel system	Mechanical pump
Lubrication system	Pressure
Cooling system	Pressure with centrifugal pump
Exhaust system	Single
Electrical system	6-volt

CLUTCH
Type	Single dry plate
Diameter	10 inches

TRANSMISSION
Type	4-speed manual plus 2-speed transfer case
Ratios: 1st	6.40:1
2nd	3.09:1
3rd	1.69:1
4th	1.00:1
Reverse	7.82:1
Transfer case, Low	1.96:1
High	1.00:1

AXLES
Type	Hypoid, full floating
Ratio	4.89:1

STEERING
Type	Worm and sector
Ratio	23.2:1

BRAKES
Service brakes	4-wheel hydraulic, internal expanding drums
Parking brake	Mechanical, external contracting drum on transmission

CHASSIS & BODY
Construction	Separate body on ladder frame
Body	Welded steel stampings
Body style	2-seat pickup truck

SUSPENSION
Front	Live axle, semi-elliptic springs (14 leaves, 39 x 1.75 inches)
Rear	Live axle, semi-elliptic springs (14 leaves, 52.25 x 1.75 inches)
Shock absorbers, front	Hydraulic, direct-acting
Rear	None
Wheels	Steel disc with split locking rim, 16 x 6.50H
Tires	9.00 x 16 eight-ply military

WEIGHTS AND MEASURES
Wheelbase	126 inches
Overall length	N/A
Overall width	N/A
Overall height	80 inches (est.)
Front track	64.8 inches
Rear track	64.8 inches
Min. road clearance	10.6 inches
Weight, empty	5,450 pounds
Gross vehicle weight	8,700 pounds

CAPACITIES
Crankcase	5 quarts (refill, less filter)
Transmission	6 pints
PTO	1.5 pints
Transfer case	3 pints
Winch worm case	1 quart
Axles (each)	6 pints
Cooling system	17 quarts (with heater)
Fuel tank	18 gallons

CALCULATED DATA
Horsepower per c.i.d.	0.40
Weight per hp	58.0 pounds
Weight per c.i.d.	23.7 pounds
Max. recom. spd.	52 mph

Right: Terrific ground clearance made Power Wagons a favorite among rural fire fighters and loggers. Facing page, top left: Front diff has a clearance of nearly a foot. Top right: Lots of fender clearance, too. Below left: Simple outside latches hold hood in place. Right: Basic instruction plaques made P.W. easy for novice to operate.

Dodge Power Wagon

built late in the war for the Chinese army.)

The T214 already had a winch up front, driven by a power take-off on the left side of the transmission. Dodge re-engineered the PTO to send power forward to the winch *or* aft to an accessory tail shaft. When ordered, the 7,500-pound-capacity Braden MU-2 winch mounted directly to the frame in front of the radiator, and wound 250 feet of 7/16-inch steel cable — just the thing for pulling freshly felled redwoods back to camp. The winch and cable alone weighed 550 pounds, requiring 14-leaf springs up front, rather than the standard 11-leaf units.

The rarely ordered rear PTO sent power via a two-piece tubular shaft to a pillow block in the center of the rear crossmember. Buyers could choose the shaft alone or, for a modest increase in price, a little gearbox that turned the direction of rotation 90 degrees to drive a nine-inch pulley. All Power Wagons came with an engine "governor" that discouraged over-revving by limiting the throttle opening; but buyers could choose a true mechanical governor that would maintain the speed of the PTO regardless of load.

Dodge offered the truck with either the 7.50 x 16 tires from the half-ton WC or the same 9.00 x 16 "high flotation" tires actually worn by military T214's. The company also offered a choice of axle ratios: the T214's 5.83:1 for serious off-road use, or the WC 1/2-ton's 4.89:1 cogs for slightly faster performance on pavement. Standard equipment included "deluxe" seats, a driver's side sun visor, and dual vacuum-powered windshield wipers — all part of a $26.65 optional "Cab Deluxe" package on Dodge's two-wheel-drive trucks.

Photos show prototypes from as early as July 1945, wearing the cab and front end described above and a standard Dodge nine-foot pickup box. But that box looked disproportionately long and low on the ex-military truck, and production versions would carry a unique box only eight feet long but 22.25 inches high. Production actually began at Dodge's Mound Road factory in Detroit in October 1945; Dodge also assembled Power Wagons in San Leandro, California, beginning in January 1946.

Only Dodge didn't call them Power Wagons, at least not in the beginning. The company announced the new vehicle as the Model WDX General Purpose Truck in the January 2, 1946 issue of *Automotive and Aviation Industries*. In February, another news item concerning its introduction appeared in a magazine called, of all things, *Power Wagon*. First published in 1906, *Power Wagon* had become a widely read trade journal for the truck industry. In March 1946, Dodge Vice President and Director of Sales Forest H. Akers used *Power Wagon* to announce that the new Dodge truck would be called, well, "Power-Wagon."

"The name... was chosen," explained Akers, "because it so aptly describes the functions of the new 94-horsepower truck; a self-propelled power plant capable of a wide range of industrial and agricultural power needs." The trucks went on sale that month, with the name Power Wagon (no hyphen this time) emblazoned in chrome on the sides of their hoods.

"It was envisioned as a farm utility vehicle, that the farmer could use to plow his fields during the week and then drive into town on the weekends," recalled Bruce Thomas, an engineer who joined Dodge in 1947. "We put it through the farm tractor tests so it could be sold in the Midwestern states where they had standards for farm tractors."

Gaskill remembers two early examples — one with a standard pickup bed, the other with a shortened wheelbase and a fifth wheel — that were shipped out, along with Raes, in May 1946 for trials on the Montana plantation of one Tom Campbell. Campbell was a friend of Chrysler President K.T. Keller, and Gaskill believes that his 68,000-acre wheat farm was the largest outside of the Soviet Union. The idea, said Gaskill, was "to turn them loose and let them find out how they would use it."

The Power Wagon never did replace the farmer's tractor; Thomas pointed out that its long wheelbase made it too difficult to turn at the end of a row of crops. Still, at least one 1947 advertisement emphasized the other farm chores

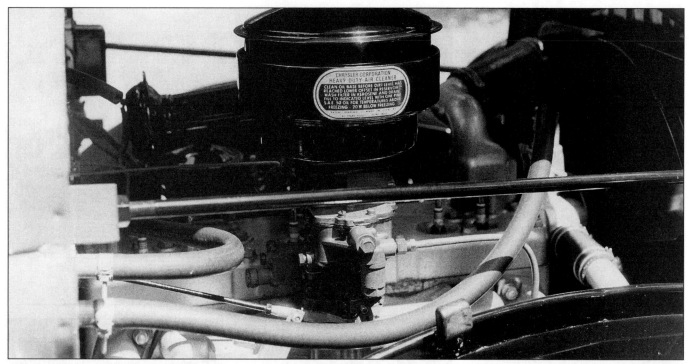

Above: Engines don't come much stronger or simpler. Below: Winch helps in tight spots. Right: Nothing fancy, but accessory armrest was available. Facing page, left: Central lever engages four-wheel drive. Right: Everything you need to know right in front of you.

Dodge Power Wagon

that a Power Wagon *could* do. "The Dodge Power-Wagon, a self-propelled power plant, makes farming easier and more profitable," read the headline. "With the tremendous traction and pulling power of its 4-wheel-drive, the Power-Wagon easily pulls two, three or more trailers." Illustrations showed the Power Wagon hauling vast loads of hay, running a saw mill and a feed grinder off its rear PTO, and stretching fence with its winch. "More and more farmers," the ad concluded, "are saying... 'the Power-Wagon is the most valuable tool on my farm.'"

And farmers did buy Power Wagons— and so did public utilities, oil fields, and fire companies. They were used as rural wreckers and even school buses. Dodge obliged by offering chassis-and-cab and, after 1950, chassis-and-cowl variations

in addition to the pickup model. Another '47 ad showed rural linemen raising a utility pole with a hoist on the front of their Power Wagon, while the copy noted how Power Wagons could run compressors, generators, even oil exploration rigs. "Thousands of 'Power Wagons' are already in use at airports, excavations, farms, ranches, forests, logging and lumber operations, mines, quarries, oil and gas companies, municipal works, and rural fire companies," continued the copy. Some wealthy individuals even mounted custom station wagon bodies on Power Wagon chassis to create a kind of ultimate hunting vehicle. The various engineering shops around Detroit built several of these, with one particularly attractive example coming from Cantrell.

Power Wagons changed over the years, though subtly, almost invisibly. Nineteen forty-nine brought a heavier-duty transmission from Dodge's one-and-a-half-ton F-series truck. More changes

arrived in 1951 than any other single year, including rubber mountings for the engine, box, and cab; a more powerful starter and fuel pump; and higher-capacity axles. Accessory gauges moved to the center of the dash for commonality with the Dodge B-series pickup. The bed changed in '51, too, from the eight-pocket type you see here to one with six smaller, tapered stake pockets and a plain tailgate.

The carburetor and governor were redesigned for 1952; and the compression ratio raised to 7.0:1 in '53 and again to 7.25:1 in '54, with a new manifold and longer-duration cam. '54 was also the last year for production in San Leandro, which had never built more than a few hundred Power Wagons annually, anyway. Twelve-volt electrics and another new bed arrived in '56, along with an optional radio—which was discontinued for '57. Some sources say that power steering and brakes joined the option list in the mid-fifties as well.

Meanwhile, Dodge totally revamped the rest of its light-truck line in 1948 and again in 1954. Then, in 1957, Dodge reached for a broader 4x4 market by offering four-wheel drive—and the Power Wagon label—on its standard three-quarter-ton and one-ton pickups. "The intent was to supersede the old Power Wagon with a new Power Wagon built using the then-current Dodge sheet metal," Thomas recalled. "But the people who really needed Power Wagons—like the forestry service and the utilities—didn't want the civilian sheet metal. The sheet metal of the original Power Wagon was so rugged, and if you did bend a fender you could just straighten it out."

"We wanted to get out of the business," confirmed Gaskill, "but people kept wanting to buy them." And for that reason the old Power Wagon remained in production, alongside the new Power Wagon, for more than a decade. Dodge debuted another all-new pickup in 1961 (again available in a "Power Wagon" version), and finally laid the old 230-c.i.d.

flathead to rest; so from '61 on, old-style Power Wagons were motivated by the 251-c.i.d. flathead six from Dodge's medium-duty trucks. Locking front hubs finally arrived in '62, followed by a stiffer standard suspension in '63. *Power Wagon*, the magazine, mailed its last issue in March of that year, but its namesake rumbled on.

Still, the original Power Wagon was playing to an ever smaller and more specialized audience, and when the Federal government passed emissions regulations for trucks, Dodge simply couldn't justify the cost of bringing the old Power Wagon into compliance. "We didn't want to re-engineer the Slant Six into it,"

Uncle Sam's Dodges

Dodge vehicles have served the US military since 1916, when General John T. Pershing used 250 Dodge touring cars to chase Pancho Villa around northern Mexico. Those Dodges performed so well that the Army ordered 7,400 more in 1917, for the big war Over There. In fact, the Ordnance Department converted 1,012 of those into the first known Dodge pickups. Later on, in the mid-twenties, the Quartermaster Department began to experiment with "Light Cross Country Cars" based on stripped-down Dodge chassis. That was the program that led ultimately to the Jeep.

President Franklin Roosevelt's administration de-emphasized specialized military trucks in favor of modified commercial designs that could be produced in greater quantity. Dodge had supplied half-ton and one-and-a-half-ton two-wheel-drive trucks since 1931, and by 1937 Dodges comprised somewhere between one third and one half of the Army's total fleet of 11,600 trucks. In 1938, Dodge opened a new plant on Mound Road in Detroit dedicated exclusively to truck production; 400,000 vehicles would roll through its gates before the end of the second world war. (Pekin Wood Products, the Helena, Arkansas, firm that had laminated the ash framing for Chrysler Town and Country bodies before the war, now shipped wooden crates to Mound Road so the trucks could be packed for export.) Partly because of Mound Road's prodigious output, plant manager L.J. Purdy was promoted to vice president in charge of Dodge Trucks.

The *first* world war had proven that an army couldn't rely on roads alone; a motorized division needed the ability to roll across open country. But four-wheel-drive was still exotic technology in the early thirties. It was Dodge, in 1934, that developed a simple 4x4 version of its one-and-a-half-ton H-30 truck, using a modified rear axle up front to reduce cost and complexity. A transfer case could uncouple the front axle to save wear on paved roads—another Dodge innovation. Dodge had shown how to build a 4x4 version of virtually any rear-

wheel-drive truck—and invented modern four-wheel-drive in the process.

The success of the Dodge one-and-a-half-ton 4x4 on soft ground and rough terrain led the Army to seek bids for a smaller, half-ton 4x4. Dodge responded with a four-wheel-drive version of its new (for 1939) commercial one-ton pickup—arbitrarily down-rated to a half-ton. This was the Dodge Model VC of 1940, and the Army ordered somewhere between 3,400 and 5,000 of them with a variety of bodies, including pickups, panel trucks, ambulances, and even a phaeton dubbed the Command Car. But the most popular VC of all was the innovative "weapons carrier"—a sort of military roadster pickup with a soft top, folding windshield, and no doors—designed to carry a gun or mortar. Ultimately, firing a gun from the back of a truck proved impractical, but the weapons carrier turned out to be incredibly useful for carrying just about everything else, even an eight-man infantry squad. And the name stuck.

Had Achilles' mother driven a VC, however, she would have dipped it in the River Styx while holding its bulky and fragile front-end sheet metal. The Army worked with Dodge to design the 1941 WC, a somewhat retro-looking alternative with skirtless, open fenders and a sturdy radiator grille that doubled as an integral brush guard. All of the VC body styles were carried over, plus a station wagon that the Army called a Carryall (and to hell with GM's rights to the name). Some ambulance versions saw action as late as the Korean War. One '41 WC ambulance saw a different kind of action even later, as a mobile prop in the television series *M*A*S*H.*

Again, however, the brass sent Dodge back to the drawing board, and Dodge returned in late '41 with the WC three-quarter-ton, a.k.a T214. Despite sabotage by enemy agents, Mound Road built some 255,000 T214's through 1945, more than half of them weapons carriers. Nearly a quarter were ambulances. T214's, particularly the weapons carriers, were also used

by our allies, including the Soviets. Interestingly, while there was no pickup version of the T214, the weapons carrier featured a full-width bed, presaging the swept-side pickups that would not appear on the civilian market for another dozen years.

In 1943, the Army boosted the size of a standard infantry squad from eight men to twelve, and Dodge responded with the T223, a 1-1/2 ton 6x6 made by adding some stretched sheet metal and another driven axle to a T214 weapons carrier. A curiously prophetic advertisement in the October 16 issue of Colliers headlined the T223 as the Dodge "Battle Wagon." In fact, the six-wheeler's anemic power-to-weight ratio limited its usefulness. Still, the Army bought 43,278 of them. The T214 and T223 neatly filled gap between the quarter-ton Jeep and the Army's larger tactical vehicles, which comprised two-and-a-half-ton trucks by GMC, International, and Studebaker; four-ton Diamond T's; and six-ton models by White and Corbitt.

By the time the T223 debuted, however, shortages of steel and rubber hampered truck production—and since it had become clear that there would be no fighting in North America, the military began to ease back on its purchases. In February 1944, the Army cut truck orders 33 percent.

After the war, a few civilian-model Power Wagons were conscripted into military service. But the Army demanded a smoother-riding, better-handling truck, and Dodge obliged with the M37 of 1950. Based on the Power Wagon, but more sophisticated and expensive, the M37 lasted through 1963. It was superseded then by the more cost-effective one-and-a-quarter-ton Jeep M715—essentially a Gladiator pickup in fatigues. (Meanwhile, the old T214 enjoyed its own 15 minutes of Hollywood fame—as the truck that finally rounds up the rhino in Howard Hawks's *Hatari!)*

But that wasn't the end of Dodge's long relationship with Uncle Sam; in 1976-77, the military ordered some 40,000 bone-stock Dodge D200 and W200 pickups.

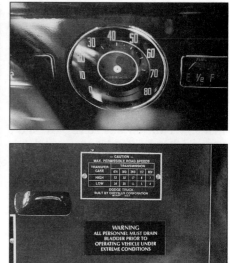

Above: *Pickup bed capacity is enormous.* **Top right:** *DriveReport truck has never seen the far side of 50 mph.* **Above right:** *Fair warning to all who enter.*

Model Numbers, Prices, and Production

The Power Wagon's official model number changed far more over the years than the actual truck ever did. This is because Dodge introduced new numbering schemes for all of its trucks in 1948, '54, and '57 — the same years that the Division debuted an all-new or extensively restyled pickup. So here are the official numbers for the Power Wagon, matched to their corresponding model years — along with base prices (with cab and pickup box) and production where available.

	Model	Price	Production
1946	WDX	$1,627	*
1947	WDX	$1,764	7,110
1948	B-1-PW	$2,045	4,960
1949	B-1-PW	$2,045	3,780
1950	B-2-PW	$2,045	4,436
1951	B-3-PW	$2,170	4,304
1952-53	B-3-PW	$2,353	8,100
1953	B-4-PW	$2,307	3,922
1954	C-1-PW	$2,307	5,473
1955-56	C-3-PW	$2,449	5,000
1956 C-4-PW		$2,449	2,794
1957	K6-W300	$2,636	**
1958	L6-W300M	$2,850	
1959	M6-W300M	$3,197	
1960	P6-WM300	$3,239	
1961	R6-WM300	$3,515	
1962	S6-WM300	$3,515	
1963	WM300	$3,531	
1964	WM300	$3,531	
1965	WM300	$3,555	
1966	WM300	$3,587	
1967	WM300	$4,295	
1968	WM300	$4,634	

*included in 1947 production
**production figures not available after 1956, but probably very small after Dodge introduced the 4x4 "Power Wagon" version of its standard pickup in 1957.

Dodge Power Wagon

Thomas explained, "because the development costs would have been very high." Never anxious to obey its own rules, the government issued variances and extensions so that it could go on buying Power Wagons for its own use. "The forest service pleaded the case that these vehicles were not used in urban areas," recalled Thomas, "and the amount of emissions they put out was infinitesimal." Ultimately, however, the EPA prevailed over its internecine rivals, and domestic Power Wagon sales ended with the 1968 model year — although Dodge shipped Power Wagons overseas for nearly a decade after that.

Ironically, Dodge developed a Slant-Six installation for the Power Wagon, anyway. Power Wagons were built under a licensing arrangement in Israel, and the Israelis wanted the newer engine to simplify parts inventories. Thomas recalled that Dodge engineers hand-built one bright-red, Slant-Six-powered prototype and then handed the drawings over to the Israelis — and let them worry about the cost of re-tooling. But overhead-valve Power Wagons were built in Israel for several years — and a few even found their way home to America. ◌

Acknowledgments and Bibliography

Don Bunn & Tom Brownell, Dodge Pickups History & Restoration Guide; *John A. Gunnell (editor),* Standard Catalog of American Light-Duty Trucks; *T. Richards (editor)* Dodge Military Vehicles Collection No. 1 *(Brooklands).*

Thanks to Mike Fleig of Vintage Power Wagons in Fairfield, Iowa; retired Chrysler engineers Roger Gaskill and Bruce Thomas; Chrysler designer and historian Jeffrey I. Godshall; Jeep Business Operations Executive Glen House; Kim M. Miller of the AACA Library and Research Center; and, of course, special thanks to owner Bill Garland.

BLUEPRINTS

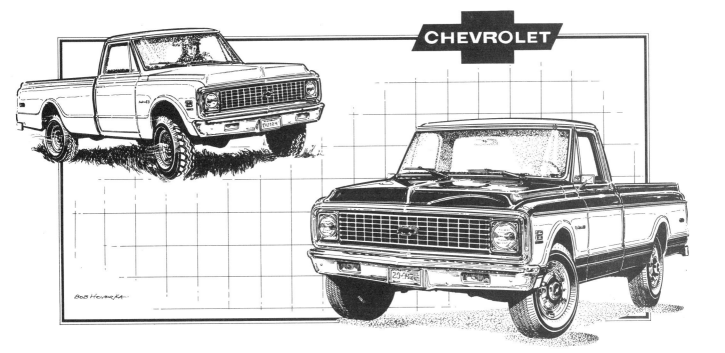

CHEVROLET

THEY were a kind of transition be-tween the stark work trucks of the forties and early fifties and the plush luxo-cruisers of the eighties and nineties. Geared more towards heavy usage, two-wheel-drive models featured independent front suspension with "heavy girders, beefy coil springs, muscular control arms." Four wheelers relied on tried and true solid axles with leaf springs.

In the half-ton "Series 10" and three-quarter-ton "Series 20," two-stage rear coils handled the load. The one-ton "Series 30" carried two-stage leaves out back. For those Series 10 and 20 owners who didn't believe the rear-mounted coils were up to the job, "You can order leaf springs for any Series 10 or 20 truck."

No-frill base models were called "Custom." They had so few amenities that brochures highlighted a vinyl-covered padded seat and molded door panels, along with a "chrome-plated" left-hand mirror. Three other packages— "Custom Deluxe," "Cheyenne" and "Cheyenne Super"—each added successive interior upgrades and additional exterior bright work. By the time you

reached the top of the line "Cheyenne Super," you had "a full seven-inch thick" bench seat upholstered in nylon cloth and "supple" vinyl. Bucket seats were optional, but dashboards received "full-gauge instrumentation" and simulated wood-grain panels. Floors were carpeted and there was even an "acoustical head-liner." "Fleetside" models, the ones with smooth rear fenders, carried upper and lower body side moldings. The separate fendered "Stepsides" did without the extra outside glitter.

Sitting behind the massive steering wheel, it's easy to see why these trucks are so popular. First: They're solid! Big round gauges reside in a steel dash-board with a huge metal glove box door. There's a bank vault feeling that just can't be duplicated with soft, curvy plas-tic. The optional radio—AM or AM/ FM—sits right in the middle, with big round knobs to turn it on and off or change the station. Even the push-but-tons are full size—no tiny micro switch-es here.

Ignition keys hang right there on the dash. A turn to the right starts a wide variety of engines, from a base 250-cubic-inch six, to an optional heavy-

duty 292 six in Series 20 and 30. V-8s begin with a 307-cubic-inch small block, move up to 350 cubes, then on to a 402 big block that Chevy labeled the "400."

Coupling semi-floating rear axles in series 10, and full floaters in Series 20 and 30, were column-shifted three-speeds in both half- and three-quarter tons. A floor-shifted four-speed was available, "and recommended for off-road use and other severe duty." It was standard in Series 30 trucks. For those who didn't want to push clutches and move levers, a pair of GM's Turbo-Hydra-Matics made the moves.

Stopping all this steel was a set of power-assisted front discs and rear drums on Series 20 and 30; half-ton drivers had to rely on the strength of their right leg unless they paid extra. Power steering was extra across the board.

But even without the niceties we take for granted today, they look good and are fun to drive. The contrast of their sharply creased hood and softly round-ed fenders is a blend that just plain works. Looking at them, it's hard to believe they're old enough to qualify for antique plates. ᐲ

1956 DODGE HALF-TON EXPRESS

THE DRIVER GETS A BREAK

DODGE Trucks' 1956 sales pitch was, "A better deal for the man at the wheel." The slogan represented a major shift in marketing strategy, for the emphasis at Dodge had always been upon ruggedness and dependability. The driver's comfort—as was true of most truck manufacturers—had been a secondary consideration at best, and with the exception of 1933–38, when some passenger car sheet metal was used on the light commercial vehicles, scant attention had been paid to styling.

Dodge had been building trucks as far back as the World War I era, when some of their vehicles had given an excellent account of themselves in military use. The tough, slow-turning, four-cylinder flathead of the early Dodge Brothers automobile had been ideally suited for use in light- and medium-duty trucks, and from 1921 to 1928 it powered the trucks produced by the Graham Brothers organization, as well as those bearing the Dodge Brothers name.

By Josiah Work
Photos by the author

The Dodge-Graham alliance had proven to be a felicitous one. Graham became the largest exclusive builder of trucks in the world, and in time—after selling a majority interest in their company to Dodge—the three Graham brothers became directors of the Dodge Brothers organization. That association was terminated in 1926, however, and the following year found the Grahams engaged in the development of the handsome new line of passenger cars that would bear their name.

Meanwhile, Walter P. Chrysler had entertained the hope of adding Dodge to his rapidly expanding automotive empire. The Chrysler Corporation's overtures were rejected initially by the Dodge Brothers directors, however, and

the resourceful Walter Chrysler had undertaken to develop a new line of trucks under the Fargo name.

Then, suddenly, Dillon Read, the investment firm that had purchased Dodge in 1925, capitulated, and on July 31, 1928, Dodge Brothers became a unit of the Chrysler Corporation. For a time, the two lines of trucks—Dodge and Fargo—were continued in parallel production. But by the close of 1930 the Fargo had disappeared from the American market. Thenceforth, the Chrysler Corporation would look to its Dodge Division for its commercial vehicles, though a few light trucks were marketed under the Plymouth name, between 1937 and 1942.

By the mid-fifties some of the competition—notably Chevrolet, with its handsome Cameo Carrier (see page 16)—had begun to pay greater attention to styling. There had been a change of design philosophy at Chrysler, too, as reflected in the handsome new Exner-

Left: V-8 emblem dominates Dodge's nose. Engine was plucked directly from the '55 Plymouth cars for use in Dodge trucks. *Below:* Front-end styling speaks more of no-nonsense utility than great beauty.

designed passenger cars of 1955. And so, in 1956, with the introduction of the re-styled C-3 series, Dodge trucks began to feature what the copywriters called "Pilot-House" cabs, appealing to the buyer's aesthetic sense as well as to the driver's comfort and convenience.

• Seats were wider, providing 61.75 inches of hip room.

• Foam rubber padding over coil springs gave a new level of seating comfort.

• Handsome, color-keyed fabrics enhanced the appearance of the optional Custom and Custom Regal cabs.

• A wraparound windshield measuring 1,023 square inches gave greater forward visibility. Custom and Custom Regal cabs even provided wraparound rear windows, achieving what the company called "full-circle" visibility and adding an attractive styling touch.

• There was even an optional automatic transmission, Chrysler's familiar two-speed Powerflite, for those who preferred not to shift for themselves.

With ratings ranging from one-half to four tons, Dodge essentially blanketed the commercial vehicle market. A choice of two engines was offered for the half-ton units. One was the venerable 230.2-cubic-inch flathead six, rated at 110 horsepower. First introduced in the 1942 Dodge passenger cars, it was a tough old workhorse—if an unspectacular performer. The second engine, which added $120 to the price of the truck, was a thoroughly modern, short-stroke V-8. Producing 169 horsepower from 259.2 cubic inches, it had been borrowed from the 1955 Plymouth passenger cars. Coincidentally, the 3.9625-inch x 3.25-inch bore and stroke of this Plymouth-cum-Dodge V-8 were identical to those of the then-current Studebaker V-8, though the latter was rated at 185 horsepower. Since the Mopar engine carried—by a narrow margin—the higher compression ratio of the two, one has to suspect that Dodge may have

rated its engine's output somewhat conservatively.

Similarly, the buyer could choose from an array of five transmissions. Standard was a three-speed manual gearbox with synchronized second and third gears. A heavy-duty three-speed was available at extra cost, as was a heavy-duty four-speed. "Shiftless" drivers could opt for the Powerflite, while those who covered a lot of highway miles could specify an overdrive if they so desired.

The half-ton models were available in several configurations, fitted to two different chassis lengths. Utilizing the 108-inch wheelbase were the pickup and a panel delivery, the latter pretentiously entitled the Town Panel. There was even a Town Wagon, which was simply a Town Panel fitted with windows and seating for eight passengers.

Mounted on a wheelbase of 116 inches, in addition to flatbed and stake bodies, was the Express, which in plain English was a long-bed pickup. Better proportioned than the rather stubby

1956 DODGE

Driving Impressions

pickup, the Express was—at least to many observers—the handsomest of all Dodge trucks for 1956—especially when fitted with the wraparound rear window. And, of course, its 90-inch bed —nearly a foot longer than that of the pickup—gave it substantially greater

utility at only a nominal increase in price.

Alan Buchner's 1956 Dodge Series C3 Express has been a "working" truck all of its life, and it is still in regular service as Alan's shop vehicle. Accordingly, we photographed it in "working" surroundings, partly at the Fresno (California) city corporation yard and partly at Fresno's Chandler Airport, where

Buchner operates an aviation specialty service.

Alan has owned the Dodge since 1965, when his father accepted it in payment for an overdue bill owed by its original owner, a crop-dusting contractor. Sound and solid, the truck had logged only 51,000 miles at that time. To that total, another 109,000 has since been added,

Over the years, a number of modifications have been made to the Express, the most obvious being a set of 15-inch wheels, complete with a set of handsome, if non-authentic, wheel covers. Clearly those covers were not intended for use on a Dodge, but no matter; the effect is very attractive. And double-oversize rear tires compensate for the "underdrive" effect of the smaller wheels. Other upgrading measures include carpeting, a 12-volt electrical system and an in-dash tape deck.

Under the hood are a couple of novelty items. Replacing the original "air-note" horn (to use Dodge's optimistic term for a device that sounded like a dying bovine) is a 1929 Klaxon, which turned up among Alan's grandfather's possessions. And for informal occasions there is a "wolf whistle."

At 120,000 miles, Buchner rebuilt the V-8 engine, overhauled the transmission and installed a new clutch. But repairs have been minimal over the years, he reports. A cosmetic restoration

Price List: 1956 Dodge Half-Ton Trucks

	6-CYLINDER	8-CYLINDER
108-Inch Wheelbase		
	BL6-108 Series	
Pickup, 17" Low-Side	$1,367	
	B6-108 Series	**B8-108 Series**
Chassis, flat-face cowl	$1,084	$1,204
Chassis and cab	$1,321	$1,441
Pickup, 17" low-side	$1,407	$1,527
Pickup, 22.5" high-side	$1,420	$1,540
Town Panel	$1,630	$1,750
116-inch Wheelbase		
	B6-116 Series	**B8-116 Series**
Chassis, flat-face cowl	$1,098	$1,218
Chassis and cab	$1,334	$1,454
Express, 17" low-side	$1,433	$1,553*
Express, 22.5" high-side	$1,446	$1,566
Stake, 7.5 foot	$1,512	$1,632
Platform, 7.5 foot	$1,446	$1,566

* DriveReport subject
(Prices are f.o.b. factory and are exclusive of excise tax and handling charges.)

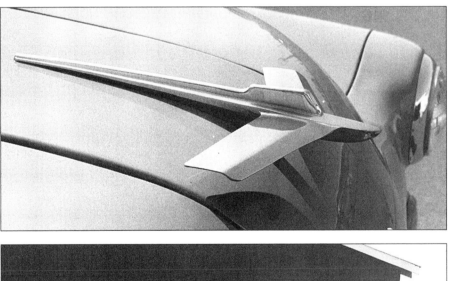

Above: "Job-Rated" slogan has appeared on Dodge trucks for many years. **Left:** Unlike '56 Dodge passenger cars, the trucks use a true wraparound windshield. **Below:** Airplane-style hood ornament adds flashy and incongruous touch to the workhorse. It looks like it belongs on a three-tone convertible instead! **Bottom:** Side profile is very square and purposeful.

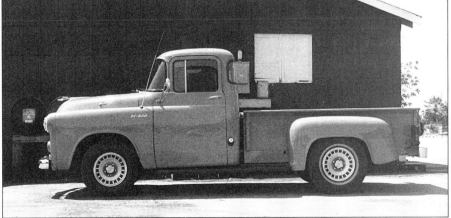

was undertaken by Alan himself in 1981, and today the truck's appearance is probably better than new!

For one thing, $120 worth of full-length oak planks has been installed on the floor of the bed. Alan protects the flawless finish of the beautiful hardwood by covering the bed with a piece of carpet whenever the Dodge is used for utility duty.

Dodge offered four trim levels for its truck cabs in 1956: Standard, Deluxe, Custom and Custom Regal. Buchner's truck has the Custom trim, a package which includes—in addition to the wraparound rear window—a foam rubber seat cushion and backrest, sound-deadening material on the floor and cab back panel, ash tray, simulated leather inside door panels and assorted other amenities. (The Custom Regal cab was gussied up even further, with bright windshield moldings, chrome-plated hooded headlamp rims, dual horns and perforated headlining.)

In terms of performance, this Dodge fairly sparkles! The factory claimed zero-to-60 acceleration in 17 seconds, which is pretty swift for this type of vehicle. Yet this truck moves out so rapidly that we wonder if the factory figures might have reflected the use of taller gears than the 4.1:1 ratio installed in this particular unit! There's so much torque that, with no load in the cargo area, it's not easy to

specifications

58.625 inches

116.0 inches

1956 Dodge C-3 Express

Original price	$1,553 f.o.b. factory, with standard equipment
Std. equipment	Oil bath air cleaner; double-acting telescopic-type shock absorbers; dual electric windshield wipers; ventilating wings; single air-note horn
Options on dR car	Custom cab equipment; heater/defroster; 4-speed heavy-duty transmission with heavy-duty clutch; directional signals; oil filter; exterior mirror; heavy-duty rear bumper; hood ornament

ENGINE

Type	V-8
Bore and stroke	3.563 x 3.25
Displacement	259.2 cubic inches
Valve config.	Ohv; hydraulic lifters
Main bearings	5
Bhp @ rpm	169 @ 4,400 gross; 134 @ 4,400 net
Torque @ rpm	243 @ 2,400 gross; 218 @ 2,000 net
Compression ratio	7.6:1
Induction system	1-2 bbl (1.43-inch) downdraft carburetor, mechanical pump
Exhaust system	Single
Electrical system	6-volt originally, now converted to 12-volt

CLUTCH

Type	Single dry disc, heavy duty
Diameter	11 inches
Actuation	Mechanical, foot pedal

TRANSMISSION

Type	4-speed heavy duty
Ratios: 1st	6.68:1
2nd	3.10:1
3rd	1.69:1
4th	1.00:1
Reverse	6.25:1

DIFFERENTIAL

Type	Hypoid
Ratio	4.1:1
Drive axles	Semi-floating

STEERING

Type	Worm and roller (aft type)
Ratio, gear	18.2:1
Ratio, overall	21.4:1
Turns, lock to lock	4.75
Turn circle	41 feet

BRAKES

Type	Hydraulic, drum-type, bonded lining
Drum diameter	11 inches
Total braking area	184 square inches

CHASSIS & BODY

Frame	6.06 x 2.03 x .156 channel side rails; 2.643 section modulus; 6 crossmembers
Body construction	All steel
Body style	1/2-ton Express

SUSPENSION

Front	Solid axle; 42-inch x 1.75-inch semi-elliptic, 7-leaf springs
Rear	Solid axle; 52-inch x 1.75-inch semi-elliptic, 6-leaf springs
Tires	6.50/16 stock (15-inch presently used)
Wheels	Drop-center steel disc, safety 4.5-inch rims

WEIGHTS AND MEASURES

Wheelbase	116 inches
Overall length	193.625 inches (202.625 inches with rear bumper)
Overall height	74.125 inches
Overall width	79.75 inches
Front tread	58.625 inches
Rear tread	61.25 inches
Ground clearance	10 inches
Shipping weight	2,850 pounds
Maximum payload	1,875 pounds

BOX MEASUREMENTS

Inside length	90 inches
Inside width (max)	48.25 inches
Height	17 inches to top of sides
Capacity	36 cubic feet

INTERIOR CAB DIMENSIONS

Hip room	61.75 inches
Shoulder room	58.375 inches

CAPACITIES

Crankcase	5 quarts (6 quarts w/filter)
Cooling system	19 quarts (20 quarts with heavy duty cooling system)
Fuel tank	17.4 gallons

Floating grille bars give truck a customized look.

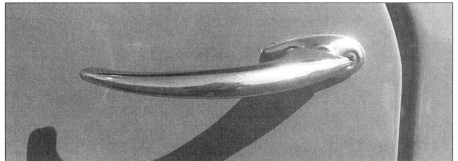

Left: 259-c.i.d. V-8 provides more than adequate motive power. *Below:* Simple, turn-type door handles rather than push-button style lend a pre-war touch to the Dodge. *Bottom:* Modern accessory-style wheels have been added to driveReport truck.

1956 DODGE

avoid wheel-spin on wet pavement, even when starting in second gear!

The ride is a little bouncy when the bed is empty, but a couple of cases of motor oil placed just inside the tail-gate—about 80 pounds in all—is enough to smooth it out quite nicely.

The clutch is smooth and pleasantly light, perhaps too light for heavy-duty use. The four-speed transmission is stiffer than a typical passenger-car gearbox, and it's easy to override the synchronizers if the driver isn't careful. First gear is a stump-puller, a genuine "granny" gear, not needed in normal driving. In fact, even third gear supplies enough torque for the Dodge to take off easily from rest.

On the other hand, Buchner complains that the overall gearing is too low—that is, numerically high—for optimum operating economy. An overdrive, coupled to the regular three-speed transmission, would have been more appropriate to the kind of duty this truck normally sees. As matters stand, the Dodge delivers only about 12 miles to the gallon in either highway or suburban service.

Steering, when the truck is at speed, is light and fairly precise. The Express goes where it is pointed, and very little road shock is transmitted to the driver's hands. Cornering takes a lot of wheel-winding, however—nearly five turns, lock to lock. And parking can be a real chore: at rest it takes a lot of muscle to turn that steering wheel.

Buchner refers to the accelerator as "short-coupled." We say it's "touchy"! Just a little pressure, and the truck is off like a shot! After a few minutes' practice, it's easy enough to control, but the action of the loud pedal isn't really one

1956 Comparison Table
Dodge ½-Ton Express vs. Chevrolet ½-Ton Pickup

	Dodge	Chevrolet
Wheelbase	116 inches*	114 inches
Cab-to-axle dimension	48 inches*	39½ inches
Engine type	Ohv V8	Ohv V8
Bore and stroke	3 ⁹⁄₁₆″ x 3¼″	3¾″ x 3″
Displacement	259.2 cubic inches	265.0 cubic inches
Horsepower @ rpm	169 @ 4,400	155 @ 4,200
Torque @ rpm	243 @ 2,400	251 @ 2,000
Compression ratio	7.6:1	7.5:1
Axle ratio, standard	4.10:1	3.90:1
Axle ratios, optional	3.74:1; 4.78:1	4.11:1
Effective braking area	174.6 square inches	158.0 square inches
Tire size (standard)	6.50/16	6.70/15
Front axle rating	2,500 pounds	2,200 pounds
Rear axle rating	3,300 pounds	3,300 pounds
Maximum gross vehicle weight	5,100 pounds	5,000 pounds

* Dodge's standard pickup used a 108-inch weelbase and measured 40 inches cab-to-axle. Other specifications as above.

Above: Centrally located glove compartment is a nice, big box. Right: Full instrumentation is standard. Below: Another old-timey touch, simple flip-up hood latches.

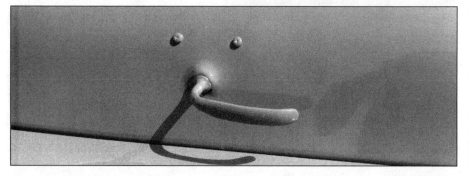

1956 DODGE

of the Dodge's better features.

We drove the Express at speeds in excess of 70 miles an hour, with lots of throttle left. Top speed must be well over 90! The engine is busy but uncomplaining at high speeds. Driven more moderately, the truck is unexpectedly quiet—partly, no doubt, due to the sound insulation of the custom cab (along with the carpeting that Alan installed), and partly because the V-8 engine is fitted with hydraulic valve lifters. Acceleration at passing speeds verges on the spectacular. We confess to some surprise at the level of performance Dodge managed to extract from a relatively small engine!

Cornering is nice and flat, even when the Dodge is pushed fairly hard. And with the extra weight of those two cases of oil at the aft end of the cargo area, the truck handles even big bumps with aplomb. The springing—semi-elliptics all around—is firm, as befits a vehicle of this type, yet we found the ride to be unexpectedly comfortable.

The brakes, which require only rather moderate pedal pressure, also give an

Continued on page 57

Option List (Partial), 1956 Dodge Half-ton Express

Cab, Custom equipment	$47.50
Cab, Custom Regal equipment	$75.00
Tinted glass (all windows)	$14.00
Directional signals	$20.00
Mirror, interior rear vision	$2.75
Horns, dual electric air-note type	$12.40
Heater, recirculating type with defroster	$40.00
Heater, fresh air type with defroster	$60.00
Wipers, dual electric	$10.00
Oil filter	$10.00
Cooling system, increased capacity	$7.50
Generator, heavy duty	$10.00
Transmission, 3-speed heavy duty (with 11-inch clutch)	$45.00
Transmission, 4-speed heavy duty (with 11-inch clutch)	$70.00
Overdrive	$100.00
Transmission, Powerflite automatic	$165.00
Bumper, rear	$10.00

Color Gallery

Photograph by David Gooley

Photograph by David Gooley

1934 Terraplane Model K

In 1934, most Terraplane trucks rolled off the assembly line without a bed, just the cab and chassis. This two-tone red example, however, was sold complete with a pickup bed and rear fender skirts. Power comes from an 80hp, 212-cu.in. flathead straight-six that's bolted to a 3-speed manual gearbox.

Although Terraplane (under the Hudson umbrella since 1932) stopped building trucks in 1938, its 212 engine was used by Hudson through 1947.

1937 Mack Jr.

For only three short model years, the heavy-duty truck manufacturer dabbled in the light-duty truck market. Dubbed Mack Jr., these light- and medium-duty trucks were actually built by REO from 1936 through 1938 with minor trim changes. Either a four- or six-cylinder engine was available. Mack Jr. eventually evolved into the ED Series, with the most common style being a fire truck.

1938 Ford Model 81C
For 1938, the light-duty Ford trucks featured an attractive oval grille and horizontal hood louvers. Two engines were available: the econo-wise 136-cu.in. V-8 that made 60hp and the larger 221-cu.in. V-8 that produced 85hp. Three-speed transmission was standard. Fog lights, passenger-side wiper, colored wheels and a chromed rear-view mirror were among the options available.

1941 Diamond T 201
With a 229-cu.in. flathead straight-six Hercules engine, Warner T-9 four-speed manual gearbox, and a Clark R650 rear axle with a 4.62:1 gear ratio, there wasn't much the one-ton Diamond T 201 couldn't haul. Ross cam and lever steering, 13 leaf springs per wheel, and Clark cast-spoke hubs with demountable rims make up the chassis. The chrome grille and window surrounds, cigarette lighter, and clock indicate that this 1941 201 is a Deluxe model.

Photograph by David Gooley

1941 Plymouth PT-125

Not well known as a light-duty truck manufacturer, Plymouth managed to build just over 6,000 pickups in 1941. Power for this 1/2-ton hauler is a 217.76-cu.in. six-cylinder L-head that makes 95hp. Chrome headlamps, right-side windshield wiper, radio, and heater were options. Plymouth stopped building trucks prior to WWII, in 1942, and didn't resume their production until 1974, with the Trail Duster.

Photograph by David Newhardt

1946 Dodge 1/2-ton Model WC

Retaining the same basic body design as the pre-war models, the 1946 Dodge 1/2-ton had several mechanical advancements. Its GVW rating was increased to 4,600 pounds, and the 95hp, 218-cu.in. L-head Six engine now benefited from a high-pressure oil pump. Additionally, all light-duty Dodges were using cross-and-trunnion U-joints, larger brakes, and worm-and-roller steering. As with all 1946 Dodge 1/2-ton pickups, this beautifully restored red and black model uses a 3-speed gearbox and has been fitted with a vintage-style aftermarket air-conditioning unit.

1946 Hudson

Although Hudson is a name normally associated with innovative and powerful cars, the company also produced a number of light-duty trucks. From 1933 until 1938, Terraplane Trucks—a division of Hudson Motor Car Co.—built these handsome utility vehicles. However, the name was changed to Hudson Trucks from then until 1947.

Those keen on such pickups will notice that the engine found under the hood of this 1946 model is a dual-carbed 308-cu-in. Six from a 1953 Hornet and not the 92-hp, 175-cu.in. L-head straight-six with which it was equipped from the factory in Detroit. Specific options include a radio and heater, and the overdrive unit found on the base 3-speed manual transmission.

1946 Studebaker M-5

After resuming the production of civilian vehicles in August 1945, Studebaker re-introduced the 1941–45 trucks as the Postwar M-Series, which remained in production until 1948. This green M-5 pickup uses the same 169.6-cu.in. L-head straight-six that powered the company's line of cars. With a 6.5:1 compression ratio, it produces a maximum output of 80 horsepower. As with all Studebaker light-duty trucks, this 1/2-ton pickup has a 3-speed manual gearbox as standard. As far as options go, this truck has none. It is bone stock and, except for the hubcaps which are from a later model Studebaker truck, all original.

Photograph by David Gooley

1947 Crosley

"Why build a battleship to cross a river?" was a phrase often heard from Powel Crosley, owner of Crosley Motors. All of his micro vehicles for 1947, including this pickup, had a 26.5hp, 44cu.in., overhead-cam four-cylinder engine that used a hydrogen-brazed, stamped-steel block and rode on an 80-inch wheelbase. Six-inch mechanical brakes and a non-synchromesh 3-speed manual transmission are some of its other basic features.

Photograph by Richard A. Lentinello

1951 Mercury M-1

Immediately after the war and until about 1957, Ford Motor Co. produced light-duty trucks in Canada, but used the Mercury name. Whereas the Ford 1/2-ton models were referred to as F-1s, the Mercs were called M-1s. Power came from a typical 106hp, 239.4-cu.in. flathead V-8 with a three-speed, column-shifted manual transmission, just like in the Ford truck line.

Photograph by David Gooley

1952 Chevrolet

With a wider and lower stance, Chevrolet's first post-war restyling—called Advance Design—came in late 1947 and lasted through early 1955. Typical for Chevy trucks, this Antelope Beige and Aztec Brown 1952 1/2-ton pickup has a 235-cu.in., six-cylinder flathead and a three-speed manual transmission. Options such as a large sun visor, tall front grille guards and rear bumper really enhance the body.

Photograph by David Newhardt

1953 Ford F-100

Incorporating numerous design and mechanical advancements, the 1953 F-100 was Ford's most significantly changed truck since 1935. Features such as a curved windshield, new front-end styling, and a larger cab not only gave the truck a better look but also, more importantly, made it more comfortable and easier to operate. Some of its upgraded hardware includes a Spicer 44 rear axle, higher-rated front suspension, and larger front and rear springs. In addition to the standard 110-hp, 239-cu.in. V-8, this F-100 has a 4-speed gearbox with synchromesh and an optional rear bumper.

Photograph by David Gooley

1956 Chevrolet 3100

Few changes, if any, were noticed in 1956 from the previous year. This bright red 1/2-ton shortbox stepside came with a 140hp, 235.5-cu.in. Thriftmaster straight-six, though a 155hp, 265-cu.in. Trademaster V-8 was available as an option, as was a Hydra-Matic transmission. Painted rear bumper and Custom Cab two-tone interior are among its few options.

Photograph by David Gooley

1956 GMC 150

A stylish two-bar grille, thick chrome bumper, and hooded headlights mark some of the major changes to the 1955–57 GMC lineup. In addition to the new styling, GMC trucks also received V-8 power for the first time. Although a 6-cylinder was standard, this 1956 Harmony Gray 3/4-tonner uses the optional Pontiac-sourced 316.6-cu.in. OHV V-8, while a 4-speed Hydra-Matic handles the automatic shifting.

Photograph by David Gooley

1964 International

Using the same 93hp, 52-cu.in. OHV slant-four found in the Scout, the International C-series might have been underpowered for the time, but with a T-13 synchromesh 3-speed and RA-1 semi-floating rear axle, it had one of the most bulletproof drivelines of all 1960s pickups. Riding on a 107-inch wheelbase, this fully restored Farm-All International is only optioned with a heater and rear bumper.

Photograph by M. Park Hunter

1979 Dodge Li'l Red Truck

Powered by a stout small-block displacing 360 cubic inches and developing 225hp and 295 lb.-ft. of torque, this was one red-hot hauler. Available only in Bright Canyon Red with gold logo and pinstripes, other distinctive features included oak or ash wood paneling fastened with stainless steel bolts and a pair of vertical chromed exhaust pipes fixed behind the cab.

Left: *DriveReport truck earns its keep most every day, hauling for its owner's business.* **Below:** *For driver, there are few real amenities compared to the plush cabs of today's pickups.* **Below center:** *Wraparound rear window is super for visibility; will also hasten your summer tan.* **Bottom:** *Box will carry six-foot by four-foot loads with ease.*

excellent account of themselves. Dual-cylinder binders are used at the rear, and the straight-through cylinder type in front, all with bonded lining. Braking area is generous, suggesting that fading should not be a problem.

But if there is one overriding feature to this truck, it must be the cab. Tight and rattle-free, it provides the driver with superb visibility as well as unusual seating comfort. The driver sits up high, surrounded by 2,322 square inches of glass. His position is erect, comfortably so; his back and thighs well supported. This is a truck one could live with!

Styling is, of course—as the lady said when she kissed the cow—a matter of taste. At the very least, Dodge's new-for-1956 C-3 Series was the best-looking line of trucks the company had produced in many years. We've always thought the 108-inch-wheelbase models looked a little stubby, though they're certainly practical enough, but the 116-inch trucks—especially the Express—are nicely proportioned. If the design can be faulted at all, it must be for the "bull" nose. Alan's truck, however, is equipped with the accessory hood ornament, which successfully overcomes that particular design flaw. From our perspective, this is really a rather good-looking piece of machinery!

And it has certainly served Alan Buchner well, over the years! 👓

Acknowledgments and Bibliography

Roy C. Ames, "A Long Way to Loogootee," Car Collector, *April 1980;* Automobile Topics, *November 28, 1925; Dodge Division factory literature; Jeffrey I. Godshall, "The Graham Brothers and Their Car,"* Automobile Quarterly, *Vol. 13, No. 1; Thomas A. McPherson,* The Dodge Story; Motor Age, *December 17, 1925, and January 26, 1928.*

Our thanks to Don Booker, Light Commercial Vehicle Association, Dayton, Ohio; Ray Borges and Linda Huntsman, Harrah Automobile Foundation, Reno, Nevada; Don Bunn, Editor, LCVA Newsletter, Minneapolis, Minnesota; Don Butler, Detroit, Michigan; Pat Datka, American Truck Historical Society, Birmingham, Alabama; Ralph Dunwoodie, Sun Valley, Nevada; Martin L. Whitmyer, Manager, Truck Public Relations, Chrysler Corporation, Detroit, Michigan. Special thanks to Alan Buchner, Fresno, California.

Nobody's Perfect!
The Yin and Yang of the 1956 Dodge Half-ton Express

Every motor vehicle, regardless of its era, type or price, has both its strong points and its weaknesses. We'll try to summarize both the good and the bad features of the Dodge V-8 Express, as we see them.

First, the things we especially liked about our driveReport truck:

• Its lively, responsive performance. This little truck is really fun to drive!

• The marvelous visibility from that "Pilot House" cab—a great boon in terms of safety, as well as convenience.

• The unusual freedom from noise, thanks to a quiet engine and a well-insulated cab.

• The unexpectedly comfortable ride, despite the absence of independent front suspension.

• The efficiency of the short-hood design, leaving room for a 90-inch bed on a comparatively short wheelbase.

But as we've noted, nobody's perfect. Chief among the flaws we noted in the Dodge Express were:

• The numerically high axle ratio, which plays hob with fuel economy. With ratios properly spaced, the four-speed transmission should have permitted the use of relatively tall gears in the rear end.

• That four-speed gearbox is no joy to use, in any case. Shifts are stiff and clumsy, and the synchronizers, despite a recent overhaul, aren't quite up to their job.

• The slow, heavy steering. The power assist, available on Dodge's heavier trucks, would have been a highly desirable option for the half-ton units as well.

• And all that glass is a mixed blessing. Visibility is among the best we've ever experienced, but that cab can get hotter than the hinges of Hell on a blazing summer day!

• Finally, although it's not a flaw in the truck itself, we feel compelled to point out that the investment potential in a vehicle such as this one is somewhat dubious. It's no cheaper to restore than a Ford F-100, for instance, and it won't bring as much on the collector-vehicle market. All of which won't matter if the initial price is right, of course!

1979 DODGE LI'L RED TRUCK

By M. Park Hunter
photos by the author

CHEVY and Ford have dominated the pickup truck market for decades, forcing outsiders like Dodge, International, Jeep and Studebaker to innovate new product ideas if they wanted to survive. The introduction of the pint-size-Peterbilt Dodge Ram in 1994 is a case in point. A big hit when it debuted, the new Ram upped Dodge's sales immensely from seven percent of the truck market in 1993 to 22 percent for model year 1996. Now Ford's new trucks have taken on a more macho, bull-nosed look too.

This isn't the first time Dodge has aped the big rigs in a play for greater sales. Back in 1978-79, Dodge offered what seemed like the ultimate niche vehicle. Instead of a traditional workhorse, the Li'l Red Truck was flashy, muscle-car fast, and impractical. Its most prominent feature was a pair of eighteen-wheeler-style chrome exhaust stacks.

Even Dodge advertising admitted this limited edition model was a toy more than a practical truck. Sales were minuscule, but the Li'l Red Truck provided some needed pizazz in Dodge showrooms. It didn't rumble onto dealer lots unheralded, though. Dodge's boss hauler was the finished product of an unusual marketing program designed to appeal to a different sort of clientele than had previously shopped Dodge showrooms.

The market in the seventies was becoming more dependent on fashion-conscious personal-use customers, and Dodge's reputation for solid, stolid trucks was more of a liability than an asset. Things had gone badly for the division. The heavy-duty line was discontinued in 1975 after capturing barely one percent of the market. Then Dodge's medium-duty trucks were canceled in 1977.

To salvage the light-duty models,

Dodge fought back that year by marketing some trucks with styling packages specifically aimed at fashion- and fun-conscious buyers. The "New Set of Adult

Above: In case you weren't sure of the name.... *Below:* Chromed vertical exhaust tips à la the big rigs.

Toys," as Dodge called them, included the Macho Power Wagon, Street Van, Ramcharger Four by Four, and Warlock.

Special advertising explained the rationale behind these models: "... there's another equally alluring side to a truck's nature and more and more, these days,

folks are discovering what it's all about. It's called 'truckin'.' Simply put, a truck can be a fun machine too...."

The Macho Power Wagon capitalized on Dodge's reputation for tough military-specification offroad vehicles dating back to World War II. The Street Van was a bid for a chunk of the custom van movement which gained popularity in the seventies. And the Ramcharger Four by Four was an attempt to inject some style into Dodge's counterpart to the Ford Bronco, Chevy Blazer, and International Scout.

The Warlock was a fashionable take on Dodge's standard pickup truck. Available in two-wheel-drive D-150 or four-wheel-drive W-150 trim, the Warlock used a standard 115-inch wheelbase and the short Utiline six-and-a-half foot bed. Utiline boxes were mounted inside the wheels, leaving fenders exposed. This was Dodge's equivalent of flair-side or step-side styling, impractical but handsome. Engine and transmission options were standard work-a-day Dodge truck.

Where Warlock stood out was in paint and trim. Six paint colors were available, though most people remember Warlocks done up in an evil gloss black. Gold pinstriping set off the cab, fenders and bed. Small chrome running boards were installed between the back of the cab and the rear fenders, and fat Goodyear radials were mounted on chrome wheels. Wood sideboards above the bed were another funky touch. Tinted glass, a small-diameter tuff steering wheel, and vinyl bucket seats set apart the "inner sanctum" (as Dodge ads called it) from traditionally Spartan truck cabs.

The Warlock was mostly show and very little go, but adding some oomph to the adult toys didn't require great feats of engineering or imagination. The mus-

RED-HOT HAULER

cle cars had gasped their last at the beginning of the decade, their big engines strangled by emissions controls. Mild versions of those famous motors, tuned for low-end torque and low emissions, lingered on in pickup trucks.

At the same time, a loophole in EPA standards relaxed the pollution requirements for trucks with a gross vehicle weight (GVW) greater than 6,100 pounds. And Dodge was still building hot engines for the police market. Boys being boys and engineers being particularly big and rowdy boys, it didn't take the guys at Dodge long to make the connection. Dick Maxwell, head of Chrysler's Performance Planning Group at the time, called the result "the last American hot rod."

The Li'l Red Truck picked up where the two-wheel-drive Warlock left off, using the same D-150 chassis, Utiline bed, five-slot chromed steel disc wheels, and wide radial

tires. Bright Canyon Red paint was the only color available, and the gold pinstripes were simplified. Instead of sideboards above the bed as on the Warlock, the bed itself on the Li'l Red Truck was trimmed outside and in with oak or ash panels and stainless steel bolts.

On the right side of the tailgate, a red

Top: *Li'l Red Express Truck might be called a standard factory custom.* **Above:** *15 x 8 wheels were standard for '79.*

Dodge decal was applied to the wood. This is often missing from trucks where the wood has been refinished. A gold decal in the center of the tailgate read "Li'l Red Truck," while decals on the doors proclaimed "Li'l Red Express Truck." Because of the door decals, many people mistakenly referred to the truck as a Li'l Red Express.

The exterior show stoppers, of course, were those twin chrome exhausts and heat shields behind the cab. Totally functional, they gave the Li'l Red Truck a trucker chic that was entirely appropriate for the seventies. (Remember the fascination with CB radios and shows like "Smokey and the Bandit" and "BJ and the Bear"?) They also sounded mean—so much so that Dodge couldn't sell the Li'l Red Truck in some areas due to local noise ordinances.

In the cab, things were a bit more mundane. Full instrumentation, an AM/FM/MX

Li'l Red Truck

stereo radio, and the small-diameter steering wheel were standard. The standard bench seat was available in red or black vinyl. Bucket seats and air conditioning cost extra.

But the real heart of the Li'l Red Truck lay under the hood. A glance would tell anyone that the Li'l Red Truck had an extroverted motor. Chrome valve covers and an air cleaner with a chrome lid and "360 EXPRESS" label hinted at something special. Twin snorkels connected to front air intakes for cold-air induction. As *Car and Driver* reported in a November 1977 report on America's fastest cars, "One look under the Dodge's hood was enough to send Terry Cook's mind reeling back to *Hot Rod*. All the implements of power are magically back in place."

Instead of the detoxed 360-cubic-inch V-8 with a two-barrel carburetor available as an option on standard Dodge trucks, the Li'l Red Truck received the E-58 police version. Internal motor components were beefed up over the standard 360. Stiffer valve springs and dampers were borrowed from the 1968 340

V-8, and bronze-bushing 1.5:1 rocker arms were fitted. A hot 3/4-grind camshaft kept intake and exhaust valves open for 252 degrees, overlapping them for only 33 degrees.

Some prototypes used big-port W-2 cylinder heads, though it is doubtful any of these made it into production. A four-barrel Holley ThermoQuad sat atop an aluminum intake manifold. The easy breathing, catalyst-free dual exhaust system dumped through twin mufflers into the exhaust stacks. With 8.2:1 compression, the E-58 made 225 net horsepower and 295 foot pounds of torque.

If those numbers seem a little tame by the old muscle car standards, remember that they are SAE net figures and the year was 1978, the dark ages of performance. *Car and Driver* had a tough time even finding eight cars that would top 110 mph without resorting to exotics like Ferrari and Lamborghini. The two most powerful cars in their test were a 350-cubic-inch Corvette and a 400-cubic-inch Trans Am. The Li'l Red Truck's torque rating fell smack between the Corvette (260 foot pounds) and the Trans Am (320 foot pounds), while its horsepower rating beat the Trans Am by five horsepower and matched the Corvette.

To hook the E-58's power up with the ground, Dodge bolted in a modified version of their LoadFlite three-speed automatic tuned for faster, higher rpm cog swapping. This was achieved with a high-stall torque converter and a modified governor borrowed from the transmissions used on 440 Wedge cars. A limited-slip 3.55:1 rear end helped put the finishing touches to those twin strips of burnt rubber laid out on the pavement.

The most important part of the performance package: the super-stiff springs and shocks needed to bring GVW

Top: Front end is stock '79 truck. **Above:** *Rear fenders protrude slightly into pickup's bed area.*

up to 6,100 pounds and make all this catalyst-free fun legal. Since the truck itself weighed 3,800 pounds, these springs had to be rated to carry a whopping 2,300-pound load. Driven with an empty bed, as Li'l Red Trucks usually were, they made for a rock-hard ride. Even then, Dodge couldn't sell this toy in California due to that state's draconian emissions regulations which didn't allow the GVW loophole.

Car magazines swooned over the Li'l Red Truck. *Hot Rod* tested a prototype with the W-2 heads and got consistent quarter-mile times around 14.7 seconds at 93 mph. They later recorded a time of 15.77 seconds and 88.06 mph for the production model. *Motor Trend* called Dodge's most ferocious progeny an "outrageous, untrammeled, unfettered, unrestricted highway carnivore."

In *Car and Driver*'s test the Li'l Red Truck displayed amazing acceleration, whipping everything else with a 0-100 mph time of 19.9 seconds. No mean feat, given that it was up against the hottest Corvette and Trans Am of the time, as well as a 400-cubic-inch V-8 Thunderbird, four-cylinder Porsche 924, turbocharged Saab, and even a Wankel-engined Mazda Cosmo. Top speed, aerodynamically limited by the flying brick profile of the truck, was still a respectable 118.8 mph.

Other aspects of the truck's character got mixed reviews. The booming exhaust note and wind noise around the stacks produced a thundering 94 decibels of interior noise in *Car and Driver*'s test. *Hot Rod* criticized the brakes for a tendency to lock unexpectedly, while *Car and Driver* described them as powerful but warned that the stiff springs caused the rear to shimmy and skid at times. *Motor Trend* could only get a maximum of 10 mpg on the highway, due to the combination of a heavy truck and a high performance motor.

Dodge began selling the Li'l Red Truck in March of 1978, partway through the model year. Special advertising described all the extra features. Ads touted it as "the truly 'customized' pickup that'll stir excitement among even the most avid 'trick-truck' enthusiasts.... The new Dodge Li'l Red Truck will turn a lot of heads...a limited-edition pickup with chrome-plated good looks."

Because of its short 1978 model run, only 2,188 Li'l Red Trucks were sold that first year. A few equipped with air conditioning experienced overheating; a July service bulletin recommended replacing the fan and drive pulleys. Despite this problem, the Li'l Red Truck served well as a traffic builder for Dodge showrooms. Overall, 1978 was a record year for the American truck market. Dodge confidently reissued the Li'l Red Truck for model year 1979 with some minor changes.

Above: Big exhaust stacks exit just behind cab. Below: Tailgate is also wood-paneled.

specifications

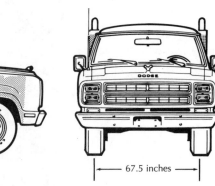

115.0 inches   67.5 inches

1979 Dodge Li'l Red Truck

Base price	$7,421.75
Price as featured	$8,045

ENGINE

Type	Cast-iron ohv E-58 V-8
Bore x stroke	4.00 inches x 3.58 inches
Displacement	360 cubic inches
Compression ratio	8.2:1
Carburetor	Holley 4160 ThermoQuad 4-barrel
Horsepower @ rpm	225 @ 3,800 (net)
Torque @ rpm	295 @ 3,200 (net)
Max. engine speed	5,800 rpm
Valve actuation	Pushrods, hydraulic lifters
Main bearings	5
Alternator	575 watts
Exhaust system	Dual 2.5-inch pipes, A134-440 mufflers, straight stacks

TRANSMISSION

Type	LoadFlite 3-speed automatic
Max. torque conv. ratio	1.90:1
Ratios: 1st	2.45:1, trans; 8.70:1, overall
2nd	1.45:1, trans; 5.15:1, overall
3rd	1.00:1, trans; 3.55:1, overall
Final drive ratio	3.55:1

STEERING

Type	Recirculating ball, power assist
Turns lock-to-lock	4.2
Turning diameter	38.0 feet

BRAKES

Actuation	Hydraulic, power assist
Front	11.8-inch vented discs
Rear	10.0x2.5-inch cast-iron drums

SUSPENSION

Front	Independent SLA, coil springs, anti-sway bar
Rear	Live axle, semi-elliptic aprings
Tire size	LR60x15
Tire type	Goodyear GT radial
Tire construction	Fabric cord, radial ply, tubeless
Wheel type	Chromed steel, 5-bolt

WEIGHTS AND MEASURES

Wheelbase	115 inches
Overall length	210.2 inches
Overall width	79.5 inches
Overall height	67.8 inches
Front track	67.5 inches
Rear track	65.2 inches
Curb weight	3,750 pounds
Weight distribution (f/r)	61.6/38.4 percent
Gross vehicle wt. rating	6,050 pounds

CAPACITIES

Fuel tank	20 gallons
Oil	5 quarts
Water	15.5 quarts

CALCULATED DATA

Weight per hp.	16.9 pounds
Output/c.i.d.	.62 bhp
Speed in gears: 1st	9.5 mph/1,000 rpm; 48 mph/5,000 rpm
2nd	16.1 mph/1,000 rpm; 80 mph/5,000 rpm
3rd	23.3 mph/1,000 rpm; 119 mph/5,100 rpm

PERFORMANCE

0-110 mph	28.8 seconds (*Car and Driver*)
Top speed	118.8 mph @ 5,098 rpm (*Car and Driver*)
1/4 mile	15.77 seconds @ 88.06 mph (*Hot Rod*)
Braking, 110-55 mph	.77 gravities (*Car and Driver*)
Fuel consumption	10 mpg (*Motor Trend*)

Sources: "Pioneer Sport Truck: Dodge's Li'l Red Express," *WPC News* (March '94); "Flat-Out in Ohio!", *Car and Driver* (Nov. '77); Chrysler promotional literature; Chrysler internal documents

Li'l Red Truck

Medium Canyon Red paint replaced the previous year's Bright Canyon Red. The '78 model had used 15x7 rims and GR60x15 tires in front and 15x8 rims with LR60x15 tires out back. No spare was included. For '79, Dodge included a spare tire and standardized all five doughnuts with 15x8 wheels and LR60x15 tires.

The grille was substantially revised, with stacked rectangular quad headlights replacing the previous year's single round lights. Parking lights moved from the grille into the area just above the bumper, and the Dodge name moved up off the grille and was spelled out in chrome letters across the hood.

Compared to the 1978 promotional literature, there was an odd lack of detailed information about the Li'l Red Truck's engine in 1979 advertisements. However, a pricing and equipment list published October 31, 1978, lists the same engine information for 1979 models as for the 1978 models. Most owners believe the 360 Express in the 1979 Li'l Red Truck was every bit as potent as the previous year's model.

Unfortunately, 1979 was a bad year to sell a gas hog. Average fuel prices had increased slowly from $.52 per gallon in 1974 to $.63 in 1978, then jumped for 1979 to $.86 per gallon. The US truck market dove 18.1 percent overall, while Dodge took a 30 percent hit. Just 5,188 Li'l Red Trucks rolled out the doors for 1979.

Dodge dropped the Adult Toys theme for 1980 and wouldn't really have another image truck until the 1994 models debuted. The 1979 slump killed other competitors, too, including International's well-respected Scout and its various custom versions like the Super Scout II and Hot Stuff pickup.

But the idea of a muscular sport truck lived on, as evidenced by the Chevrolet 454 SS built from 1989-1993 and the Ford F-150 Lightning introduced in 1993. And the hordes of customized pickups crowding modern highways are another tribute to the durability of the concept. The obscure niche pioneered by Dodge in the late seventies is now a competitive market driven by image and power.

Ironically, as this market has blossomed the Li'l Red Truck has found a new and appreciative audience. Because few of these vehicles were used for work, many good examples survive. Nice ones command prices of $7,000 or more, a bargain for a vehicle with undoubted collector appeal and good performance.

Driving Impressions

Our feature truck belongs to Ed Turner of Watseka, Illinois. Although it's the slightly more common 1979 model, this particular example has a colorful history. Turner had liked the Li'l Red

Facing page: Truck has a combination of fun and no-nonsense appearance. **This page, top left:** Wood trim extends over rear fenders. **Right:** driveReport truck has standard bench seat. **Above:** 360 V-8 delivers fierce acceleration and top speed of nearly 120 mph.

Li'l Red Truck

Truck when it debuted but couldn't afford one: "I just thought they were cute when they came out in '78 and '79, but back then eight or nine thousand dollars was a lot for a truck."

In 1984, he found one in a body shop for a better price. He says, "It'd been wrecked and repainted. Somebody had made a generic 'Li'l Black Truck.' The body was black and the boards had been painted red. The rims were gone and the stacks were [replaced with incorrect pipes], but it had only 19,000 miles on it. The first couple of years it had had a hard life but not a lot of miles, but it was built like a tank so it was okay."

"The guy that wrecked it had this superficial job done," according to Turner. "Then while the truck was in the shop, he killed his wife and went to jail. The shop had a lien on it and finally got the title. It had been sitting there for a very long time."

Turner adds, "I did a lot of searching to find the parts. [Back then] you could buy the decal package and all the fender stripes. I have a spare set now to do it over again." Other parts like the correct stacks were difficult to locate, even though the truck was only five years old at the time. The original wood had rotted from the inside out, so Turner went to southern Illinois to purchase some high quality white oak and had it redone. By 1988, the

restored Li'l Red Truck was finally ready to take to shows.

The "custom-truck" appeal of this vehicle is such that many owners have added their own little touches. Turner is no exception, and his modifications are in the spirit of the truck and its era. The gold-plated ram hood ornament is non-original, as are the red dice caps on the tire valves and the "Dirty, Mean, and Nasty" mudflaps. To keep water and dirt from accumulating in the rolled edges of the bed, Turner added stainless steel caps taken from (of all things) a kitchen sink. He has also upgraded the stereo to modern standards. Modern Goodyear Eagle GTs have replaced the scarce original Goodyear performance tires.

Turner's truck is a regular at many local events and is always driven to shows, accumulating a couple thousand miles each year. Turner notes that it came from the factory built like a luxury car with cruise control and air condi-

Top: Big V-8 is good for 225 horses. **Above:** *Gauges are easy to read at speed.* **Facing page, top:** *Express Truck models are highly collectible.* **Bottom:** *Dodge has its practical side, with good carrying capacity in the wood-lined bed.*

tioning. With the heavy-duty springs and powerful engine, Turner says it is a wonderful driver and would be great for pulling trailers. He's never seen the thermometer climb even in the worst summer heat.

Not old enough to be judged with the antiques, Turner's truck often competes for the popular vote against hot rods and modern trucks. Turner says he doesn't win a lot of trophies, "but you do get a lot of comments. No one can believe it's factory. It's a great conversation piece."

My first thought upon seeing the truck is of a cartoon come to life. Everything is exaggerated: flaming red paint, big hood and cab, tiny bed, haunch-like rear fenders, meaty tires and above all those larger-than-life chrome stacks. I shouldn't be surprised. MoPar designers had a lot of experience with cartoon-like design from the days of the Road Runner and Superbird.

Somehow the Li'l Red Truck walks a line just short of being garish. The stickers and gewgaws combine to make the truck look tough with a touch of humor and nostalgia. Dodge pulled off a trick even mighty GM couldn't manage. For an example of how bad the seventies school of plastic-and-adhesive styling could be, remember the thunder chicken Trans Ams that became an instant parody of themselves.

I expected to be impressed by my first glance of the last hairy-chested gonzo American V-8. I'm not. The cavernous area under the hood makes the big 360 look small, which it isn't, and a spaghetti bowl of wires and hoses further hides the heart of the matter. The chrome valve covers and special air cleaner do promise a good time, though. Those twin snorkels have an especially aggressive look.

Turner fires up the engine and we stand outside the truck, sipping our morning coffee and waiting for it to warm up. The 360 idles with a barrel-chested rumble, puffing vapor out the exhaust pipes as overnight condensation in the stacks evaporates. During the photo session, the engine proves again and again to be a reliable starter and is surprisingly docile idling or at speed. Many performance-tuned V-8s never managed to be this civil.

The seventies were the decade that brought us polyester leisure suits and velour upholstery. The Li'l Red Truck's interior captures this luxo, macho, el cheapo flavor exactly. Synthetic carpeting, vinyl seats and plastic dash panels all masquerade as more expensive materials.

Modern critics would complain about this stuff in anything other than the cheapest economy hatchback, and it is an effort to remember that the Li'l Red Truck's interior was considered pretty swanky in its day.

At least the seats are comfortable and cushy, especially by truck standards. Visibility in all directions is great, typical of the glassy cabin and high seating position in trucks. The tuff steering wheel falls easily to hand but blocks the top of the instruments from view. Steering requires a light effort and is a fair compromise between quick but stiff and slow but mushy. The brake pedal is firm, heavy and a bit numb. The throttle is likewise very stiff, which would rapidly tire my right leg on long trips.

Step on the gas pedal hard and the engine will spin the tires, causing the rear end to slew around slightly. The LoadFlite automatic does its job with gusto, snapping off fast and smooth shifts. Acceleration is brisk, but the roar from the pipes makes the Li'l Red Truck feel even faster than it is. In addition to the noise from the stacks, there is some turbulence and air leaking into the cabin around the top edges of the doors, a common problem with Dodge trucks of this generation.

Midway through each gear, just as the power is really starting to come on strong, the 360 suddenly chokes and

stutters for a few moments. Turner blames this on the plastic-bodied ThermoQuad, a carb not known to age gracefully. Most likely, the plastic base has warped slightly and air leaks around the secondaries are putting a hitch in the truck's git-along.

The ride is very firm. For all the elasticity in those super-duty spring and shocks out back, the Li'l Red Truck might as well be suspended on two-by-four pine boards. The front end feels massive, but doesn't hammer road or driver mercilessly. To my surprise, the ride has a choppy fore-and-aft feeling usually more apparent in short-wheelbase subcompact cars. I attribute it to the high seating position and firm rear end.

In short, the Li'l Red Truck is . . . a truck, albeit a fast and flashy one. The folks at Dodge never pretended otherwise. To have made it too much like a

car would have ruined the appeal. "Truckin'" is as addictive today as it was in '78. Too bad the short supply of Li'l Red Trucks limits this pleasure to a lucky few.

In fact, after my short stint behind the wheel of Turner's unsubtle cruiser, I started dreaming. After all, Chrysler is the company that brought us the Viper and Prowler in recent years. And the Viper engine is just a souped-up aluminum version of the cast-iron V-10 truck motor. Imagine a new red Ram with chrome stacks and a Viper V-10 under the hood. Bring back the Li'l Red Truck! ᴖ

Acknowledgments and Bibliography

Articles in the following magazines were used in preparing this article: Car and Driver *(November '77);* Collectible Commercial Vehicles *(October '91);* Hot Rod *(November '77, June '78);* High Performance Mopar *(Spring '88);* Motor Trend *(April '79);* Muscle Car and Truck Buyer's Guide *(Spring '91);* WPC News *(March '94).*

Books consulted: HPBooks Auto Dictionary *(HPBooks, 1993);* The World Almanac and Book of Facts 1995 *(Funk & Wagnalls, 1994).*

Thanks to Bob Dierksheide and the Walter P. Chrysler Club for their assistance, and especially to Ed Turner for the opportunity to photograph and drive his Li'l Red Truck.

'79 Dodge Li'l Red Truck

PARTS
Li'l Red Express Parts
Michael Gress Enterprises
1525 Marsha Terrace
Yardley, PA 19067

Roberts Motor Parts
17 Prospect Street
West Newbury, MA 01985
508/363-5407 (phone)
508-363-2026 (FAX)

CLUBS
American Truck Historical Society
300 Office Park Drive **or** PO Box 531168
Birmingham, AL 35253
205/870-0566 (phone)
205-870-3069 (FAX)
(15,300 members, bimonthly magazine, library and archives, $20/year dues)

Walter P. Chrysler Club
PO Box 3504
Kalamazoo, MI 49003-3504
616-375-5535 (phone)
4,800 members, all Chrysler products, annual meet, monthly newsletter, $23/year)

1953 FORD F-100

By Dave Emanuel
Photos by the author

INTERNATIONAL Harvester has always produced the ugly duckling of pickup trucks. And on occasion, Dodge has seriously challenged IH in the competition for the Oscar of Ugly. Chevrolet, on the other hand, has designed some rather attractive pickups. Collectors seem especially fond of the Cameo series produced during the mid-fifties. But in terms of building a dedicated following, the Cameo is a distant second to the 1953–56 Ford F-100.

No other truck, and damn few cars have ever inspired the almost maniacal fervor found in F-100 aficionados. In fact, Ford's early fifties pickup is every bit as much of a "cult" vehicle as the Chevrolet Corvette or VW Beetle. Most owners feel that mere possession of one

of these automotive phenomena is not sufficient: a custom paint job complemented by a cornucopia of accessories must be lavished upon the vehicle. To do less is to commit heresy, a crime punishable by imprisonment behind the wheel of an IH or Dodge pickup.

How the F-100 came to instill such intense feelings in its followers is somewhat of a mystery, but perhaps it owes to the residual effects of "Measuring Man." A rather dapper-appearing rogue—one might consider him the strong, silent type—"Measuring Man" stood 5 feet, 9½ inches tall and tipped the scales at 166 pounds. But rather than being a creature of flesh and blood, he was wrought of plastic. His purpose in life was to assist Ford engineers in

incorporating the "human element" into the design of the cabs on 1953 Ford trucks. "Driverized" cabs, as Ford called them, were hallmarks of the all-new pickups released in March 1953, under the F-100 model designation. And although the F-100 incorporated a number of significant innovations, its lineage clearly traces back to its immediate ancestor, the F-1.

During the four years prior to the release of the '53 models, Ford truck series labels ranged from F-1 through F-8, depending upon wheelbase and gross vehicle weight (GVW) rating. Introduced for the 1948 model year, Ford launched its first truly new post-war trucks amidst much fanfare aimed at making the public aware that it wasn't just offering the same old candy bar in an updated wrapper. Sales literature proclaimed in headline-size type, "New, New, Brand-New!" and went on to note, "A Galaxy of New Engineering Ideas Pent up by War-Born Conditions. Now Yours in New Ford Bonus Built Trucks for '48." The verbiage that accompanied these headlines was equally enthusiastic. "Holding fast to all that has made the Ford Truck the Endurance Champion among the industry's sales leaders, Ford now brings you the full benefit of five years of intensive engineering research!

"These Bonus Built Trucks are all new, from grille to taillamp. But they're service-proved down to the smallest forging. You'll vote them first place in value.

"In what way? In *every* way! In power, in performance, in safety, in economy, in comfort, in rugged endurance—yes, even in the world-famed traditional Ford reliability—they're better trucks."

"Bonus" was the key word, and to ensure that no misunderstandings arose, it was noted that, "Webster's Dictionary definition of word 'Bonus' was 'Something given in addition to what is usual or strictly due.'"

For the half-ton F-1, priced at $1,212, the "Bonuses" included a standard 226-cubic-inch, 95-hp inline six or optional 239-cubic-inch, 100-hp flathead V-8. With bore and stroke measuring 3.3 inches and 4.4 inches respectively, the six, with a compression ratio of 6.8:1, produced 180 lb./ft of torque at 1,200 rpm. "Flightlight" pistons containing

Originally published in Special Interest Autos #80, Mar.-Apr. 1984

was ready for a new sales assault. The truck division's lead-off batter was the new F-100 half-ton, which, like its larger siblings, sported "Driverized" cabs to reduce driving fatigue. Ford also claimed, "New Ford *Economy* Trucks for '53 are engineered with many time- and labor-saving features to do their jobs faster, to handle more deliveries per hour, to make more trips per day. They are the sweetest-handling trucks ever built!"

The "sweet handling" was again complemented by either a six-cylinder or V-8 engine, both of which had been revised to produce increased power. Rated at 106 hp at 3,500 rpm and 194 lb./ft of torque at 1,900–2,100 rpm, the 1953 V-8 shared most specifications, including bore and stroke dimensions, with its predecessors. However, the inline six was indeed all new. With a bore and stroke of 3.56 inches and 3.6 inches respectively, displacement measured 215 cubic inches—11 less than in previously available sixes. Yet horsepower had been increased to 101, while torque rose to 185 lb./ft. The improved ratings were due to a revolutionary, for Ford, change in engine construction: overhead valves. Ford had finally begun moving away from its flathead technology.

Mated to either the standard six or optional V-8 was another first for Ford: a fully automatic transmission. And, if clutchless operation was too revolutionary for some tastes, gearbox choices included a standard three-speed or optional heavy-duty three-speed, overdrive or four-speed. Except for the four-speed, all shift levers were column mounted, "for smooth, quiet operation with passenger-car shifting ease."

While new features could be found in all quarters, Ford gave the biggest play to the "Driverized" cabs which, courtesy of Measuring Man, offered improved visibility, larger doors and a new curved instrument panel with "cockpit" cluster. The company also claimed that the new F-l00s were the "Roomiest, Most Comfortable Truck Cabs on the American Road." Sales literature also noted, "The all-new Ford *Driverized* Cabs usher in a completely new era of truck riding comfort. They ride so easily, you handle the controls so easily, you won't believe you're riding in a truck."

Taken in the context of today's social conventions, those claims could be reasonably interpreted as an attempt to lure potential female customers. But such was not the case. Thirty years ago, when a woman's place was in the home, trucks were decidedly masculine vehicles, and in its literature Ford unabashedly stated, "New Wider Seat provides roomy comfort for three men."

For 1954, Ford maintained the basic F-100 body and chassis, but incorporated a number of refinements. The "Cost Clipper" six-cylinder was enlarged to

Above left: Part of the new look was the change in tailgate lettering from the traditional Ford script to modern block letters. *Above:* Fresh air fiends were taken care of via this cowl vent. *Left:* Hubcap shape and lettering design is nearly identical to 1946 Ford passenger cars. *Below:* F-100 drivers ride tall in the saddle, with excellent visibility, good handling at their command.

Right: The final flowering of the flathead V-8. This version developed 106 bhp with modest 6.8:1 compression ratio. *Below:* Interior is functional yet bright and attractive with two-tone upholstery and matching interior/exterior colors. *Bottom:* Steering wheel boss notes fiftieth anniversary of Ford in 1953.

1953 FORD

223 cubic inches by virtue of a .060-inch increase in bore size. Combined with a compression ratio of 7.2:1, the displacement increase allowed horsepower to be bumped to 115 while torque rose to 193 lb./ft. But the big news came from the V-8 corral, where the venerable flathead had finally been put out to pasture. In its stead was an overhead-valve powerplant of the same displacement, but with dramatically altered bore and stroke dimensions. Where the flathead achieved 239 cubic inches through a 3.19-inch by 3.75-inch bore/stroke combination, its overhead valve replacement was of the modern short-stroke design: it measured 3.50 inches by 3.10 inches. Once again, horsepower and torque were up from previous years. With a 7.2:1 compression ratio, the 1954 "Power King" V-8 produced 130 hp at 4,200 rpm and 214 lb./ft at 1,800–2,200 rpm.

Ever since 1953, Ford half-ton pickups have worn the F-100 label. But in 1957 the line was once again complete-ly redesigned. At the time, the new models were significant because they marked the beginning of a new era. But looking back, they actually signaled the end of an old one.

Driving Impressions

A horse is a horse, of course, of course, unless of course, the name of the horse is Mr. Ed. Following that line of thinking, a truck is a truck, et cetera, unless of course its name is F-l00. There is something strangely appealing about the '53–'56 F-100s; like the infamous horse, the Ford pickups of this era talk to you. Not being a dyed-in-the-wool truck cognoscente, I'm not quite sure what they're saying, but I can hear the voices. And some, like the one belonging to Bob Walton's shimmering red F-100 (seen in accompanying photos), are marked by a unique accent peculiar to a breed—the flathead V-8—that became extinct at the end of the 1953 model year.

Walton, of Bellaire, Texas, evidently hears the voices too. The owner of a body shop, Bob normally performs all his own restoration work; it took something special to coax him into buying a vehicle that had already been returned to pristine condition. Strange voices have that type of power.

In Texas, trucks are used primarily on farms and ranches, so for the photo and driving sessions it seemed rather appropriate to find a location a world away from bustling Houston. I arranged to meet Walton just outside the town of Hockley, which lies about 25 miles northwest of Houston. The actual meeting site was, quite appropriately, the intersection of US Route 290 and Farm-To-Market road number 2920.

specifications

60.58 inches

110.0 inches

1953 Ford F-100 half-ton pickup

Base price	$1,330
Options on dR car	Rear bumper, outside rearview mirrors, turn signals, heater/defroster, windshield washer, oil filter, right hand taillight.

ENGINE
Type	L-head V-8
Bore & stroke	3.19 inches x 3.75 inches
Displacement	239 cubic inches
Horsepower	106 @ 3,500 rpm
Torque	194 @ 1,900-2,100 rpm
Compression ratio	6.8:1
Induction	Stromberg 2-barrel, downdraft
Exhaust system	Cast-iron exhaust manifolds, dual exhaust
Electrical system	6-volt battery/coil

TRANSMISSION
Type	3-speed manual
Ratios: 1st	2.78:1
2nd	1.62:1
3rd	1:1
Reverse	3.655:1

DIFFERENTIAL
Type	Hypoid semi-floating
Ratio	3.92:1

STEERING
Type	Worm and dual row needle bearing roller
Ratio	18.2:1
Turning circle	37.1 feet

BRAKES
Type	Hydraulic, duo-servo; cast iron drums
Front	11 inches diameter x 2 inches wide
Rear	11 inches diameter x 1.75 inches wide
Total swept area	178 square inches

CHASSIS & BODY
Construction	Welded channel frame, tapered front and rear with 4 cross-members
Body	2-door pickup cab with separate bed

SUSPENSION
Front	Modified I-beam axle with semi-elliptic 8-leaf springs and double-acting tubular shocks
Rear	Live axle with semi-elliptical leaf springs and double-acting shocks
Wheels	16-inch x 4-1/2-inch steel disc
Tires	6.00 x 16 four ply

WEIGHTS AND MEASURES
Wheelbase	110 inches
Overall length	183 inches (from front bumper to rear of frame)
Track	60.58 inches front; 60.0 inches rear
Curb weight	2,970 pounds
Payload	1,030 pounds
GWV	4,000 pounds

On a typically hot and humid July afternoon, the truck, rolling through the broad, flat expanse of Texas farmland, seemed to be carrying us through a time warp. As we traveled away from our meeting spot, sans air conditioning, the windows were rolled down and vent panes twisted opened. With no radio, and no other cars around, it could just as easily have been 1953, rather than 1983. And, rather than doing a drive-Report, we could have been returning to the ranch after delivering a load of hay, or the product of that hay after it had been processed by a horse.

But after bumping along for a few miles, my reverie shattered and reality returned. The first thing that struck me was that, in spite of all the grand verbiage Ford had put forth concerning the "Driverized" cab, the interior is actually quite Spartan. All the instruments are housed in a pod directly in front of the driver. Except for a few knobs and igni-tion switch, the dashboard sheet metal extends uninterrupted from side to side. It flows into the inner door panels, which are equally bereft of padding, covering or frills. Plain, black rubber mats maintain the Spartan feel underfoot, while two tones of unfancified vinyl carry the theme under derriere.

Juxtaposed to the less-than-glamorous cab is a pickup bed floored with beautifully finished, seasoned wood. The individual natural-toned boards are separated by steel skid strips painted black and designed to prevent sharp objects from gouging the wood, The bed itself measures 45 cubic feet and has heavy gauge steel side panels 20 inches tall.

Climbing up over the running board and into the cab, I was immediately struck by the size of the steering wheel—it measures 18 inches in diameter. As with most trucks, the seat still seems too close to the dash, even in its

*Right: Ford paid special attention to steering wheel, pedal positions and seating when designing F-100's interior. Result was better than expected comfort in a pickup truck. **Bottom:** With a base price of $1,330 in 1953, F-100 had to be one of the all-time bargains in useful, good-looking half-ton pickups.*

1953 FORD

hindmost position, and that, combined with driver positioning, further accentuates the steering wheel's size. But when it becomes necessary to make a tight turn at low speeds, the 18-inch diameter no longer seems so obtrusive, as the leverage afforded enables drivers weaned on power-assisted steering to crank the wheel.

Considering its 239-cubic-inch displacement, minuscule even by today's downsized standards, the engine, by virtue of its 3.75-inch stroke, produces healthy amounts of low-speed torque. With an overall gear ratio in first exceeding 11:1, the truck is able to easily pull away, tractor style, from a dead stop. And the relatively low speed at which maximum torque is produced enables the engine to handle the wide drops between gears with ease.

Those rpm drops are effected through operation of a clutch pedal and column-mounted shift lever—something that hasn't been seen in recent years. It is a strange anomaly of automotive design that, in the fifties, companies strove to get the lever off the floor—even in basic utility vehicles—just in time to put it back. By the early sixties (except in bread-and-butter sedans equipped with automatics), floor mounted shift levers had become quite the rage, as sportiness eclipsed utilitarianism as a major sales consideration.

In a proper pickup truck, load carrying capacity is also a major sales point, and the suspension plays an important role in determining the amount of weight that can be accommodated. The suspension also determines at what pace a vehicle can be made to clip down a winding road. Compared to the sedans of the early fifties, the F-100 is quite a handler. With no load aboard, corners can be negotiated at surprisingly high speeds with comparatively little body roll. While amply proportioned anti-roll bars may be absent, the stiff semi-elliptic leaf springs and double-acting shock absorbers that allow up to a half-ton of cargo to be carried, also keep swing and sway to a minimum. Cornering power is compromised primarily by skinny bias-ply tires, vehicle height and solid I-beam front axle.

While the ride might be rough and the interior Spartan, the F-100 can't be faulted for its honesty. It doesn't masquerade as something it isn't and can't hope to be. Its purpose in life is to transport whatever is placed in its bed with economy and dispatch, while affording driver and passengers reasonable comfort. It puts on no airs nor attempts to play more than a single role. It is plainly and simply a truck. And a very good truck at that. ൙

Acknowledgments and Bibliography

Ford sales and technical literature, 1948–1956; Paul Woudenberg, Ford: Closing the Years of Tradition; *Ray Miller,* The V-8 Affair.

Thanks to Tim Howley, Oakland, California. Special thanks to Bob Walton, Houston, Texas, and to Milton Helfrich, Hockley, Texas, for allowing SIA to roam around his farm.

If ever a truck was designed with the driver in mind...

this new Ford Truck is it! New "DRIVERIZED" Cab cuts driver fatigue!
New easy handling saves work and time getting around in tight spots!
These and many other TIME-SAVING features help get jobs done fast!

TIME IS MONEY! Today's truck owners know it. Ford Truck engineers know it. That's why TIME-SAVING was a major goal in designing the completely new Ford Trucks for 1953. With scores of new TIME-SAVING features, the new Ford Trucks are made-to-order for economical operation in today's traffic stream.

New "DRIVERIZED" Cabs provide living-room comfort, cut driver fatigue. They help save time by making driving easier.

The new Ford Truck seat is something special. Wider, of course. Non-sag seat springs. Adjustable seat cushion *and* independently adjustable back-rest. Most interesting new Ford exclusive feature is that every seat now has a built-in *shock snubber* to help level out the ride.

For easier maneuvering in tight quarters, at loading docks or in city traffic, Ford Truck turning diameter has been considerably reduced. This was done by "setting back" the front axle, widening the front tread, and by improving the steering geometry.

Synchro-Silent type transmissions are now

COMPLETELY NEW Ford Model F-100 Pickup with 6½-ft. box, features new *bolted* construction, new clamp-tight tailgate. Choice of V-8 or Six. *Five* transmissions, including FORDOMATIC DRIVE and OVERDRIVE (extra cost).

standard on all Ford Truck models . . . and at no extra cost. This means easier and faster shifting, less truck momentum lost, more time saved with faster acceleration.

Fully automatic drive is now available in Ford Model F-100 half-ton trucks at extra cost. Fordomatic is a great time-saving convenience. A gas-saving, engine-saving OVERDRIVE transmission is also available at extra cost in this model.

New short-stroke engine design releases extra power for time-saving delivery by cutting engine friction up to 20%.

You have five Ford Truck engines to choose from. Three Low Friction overhead-valve engines, the 101-h.p. Cost Clipper Six, plus the 145-h.p. and 155-h.p. Cargo King V-8's are teamed with the world-famous 106-h.p. Truck V-8 and the economy-proved 112-h.p. Big Six.

Only Ford gives you a choice of V-8 or Six in light- and heavy-duty trucks!

New Ford service accessibility saves time in the shop. Front ends have been redesigned. Hoods are wider. Frames are wider, too, per-

mitting a new fender contour that makes engines much easier to get at.

NEW GIANT of the "extra heavies." Ford F-900 carries 55,000 lb. GCW or 27,000 lb. GVW ratings.

Get the one *right* truck for your job by choosing from an expanded line of over 190 completely new Ford Truck models ranging from half-ton Pickups to the 55,000 lb. GCW Big Jobs. *There's so much more you should know about the new* TIME-SAVING *Ford Trucks . . . so much more your Ford Dealer wants to tell you. See him soon!*

Fifty Years Forward on the American Road

FORD *ECONOMY* TRUCKS
SAVE TIME! SAVE MONEY! LAST LONGER!

NEW "DRIVERIZED" CABS cut driver fatigue. Both the Standard and Deluxe Cab (shown) have new curved one-piece windshield, 55% bigger for more visibility; new 4-ft. wide rear window; new wider adjustable seat, with new non-sag springs and new *shock snubber*; new push-button door handles and new rotor-type latches.

Handsome Hauler

Advancing truck design in '49 with GMC's 3/4-ton pickup

By John Katz

Photography by Robert Gross and Vincent Wright

Advance-Design, they called it: a bold new idea in trucks, a new commitment not only to utility but to passenger comfort. Earlier light trucks had been styled to look like cars; but the ones that General Motors released in the summer of 1947 were designed to look like trucks while offering a more car-like experience for the driver and passengers. In that respect they might be considered the first modern trucks, perhaps even the harbingers of an unforeseen era, half a century

later, when Americans would buy more new trucks than cars.

Except that the Advance-Design trucks were never intended to replace cars. They were still working vehicles, and I vividly recall them still working well into the late Sixties, when they were beginning to look a bit tatty and not very advanced at all. Mostly I remember seeing the Chevrolets, whose broad, toothless grins hadn't worn well with time, particularly after hard use had knocked a grille bar or two askew. The GMCs, I

thought, looked neater, sturdier, but then as now you didn't see them as often. And not surprisingly so: In calendar-year 1949, when our driveReport truck was new, Chevrolet produced 383,543 commercial vehicles. GMC built 80,407.

The cab was shared between them, however, and the cab was the critical element in the Advance-Design concept. AD interiors stretched eight inches wider and seven inches longer than those of the previous generation, and

Originally published in Special Interest Autos #179, Sept.-Oct. 2000

GMC recommended 3,000-rpm engine speed limit.

Big wheel needed for the 26.24:1 steering ratio.

the seats adjusted like passenger-car seats, riding up on a ramp as they slid forward to give a taller view to shorter drivers. The doors, with hinges now hidden, were four inches wider for easier entry and exit, and extended at the bottom to hide the sills.

Getting in still required a big step off the ground, and I'd have been grateful for the running boards, if they weren't restored to show quality and I was actually going to use them. Once inside, I sit higher above the road than in even a late-Forties passenger car. The seat itself is indeed passenger-car comfortable and, pushed all the way back, leaves adequate leg-room for under-six-footers. The 18-inch steering wheel inclines toward the horizontal and intrudes on my personal spare-tire space, but a slimmer driver wouldn't even notice.

Visibility and ventilation were also important goals of Advance-Design, and in both categories the driveReport truck matches or exceeds contemporary passenger-car standards. The high seating

position; the broad, veed windshield with relatively slim posts; and short, sloping engine hood all contribute to a commanding view down the road. There's a screened, pop-up vent in the top of the cowl, and another in the footwell on the driver's side, and with both of them open, cool air pours into the cockpit at anything over walking speed. An old-style recirculating-air heater lingered on the option list, but our driveReport truck has the all-new, dealer-installed fresh-air heater/defroster. It breathes through a stack of horizontal louvers on the right side of the cowl, so there's no pop-out vent over there.

Large, round gauges feature dark copper numbers on a white face, although the small red pointers tend to get lost in the bold design. Choke and throttle knobs are placed high on the dash and clearly labeled; wiper and headlight controls are just as handy but not labeled at all, while heater controls are scattered across the bottom of the panel, requiring an inconvenient reach.

The engine is an overhead-valve Six, but beyond its basic configuration it shares nothing with the contemporary Chevrolet. It is actually derived from the old Buick Six; GMC Division took over its manufacture in 1931, when Buick switched to Eights exclusively. Its cylinder dimensions of 3-9/16 x 3-13/16 are unique to GMC trucks of 1939-53. It is a sturdy engine. In the days when Ford flatheads still dominated drag racing, a GMC 228 with triple carbs could blow past ol' Henry's V-8. Owner Leo Ethier said that bottom end of his has never been apart, although he did take the head off to have the valve seats coated for unleaded gas.

Simple front end has very handsome styling.

Rounded cab, separate fenders, and lack of chrome adornment looks ruggedly handsome.

A plunger in the middle of the floorboard activates the "toe-heel" starter; it's positioned so you naturally stomp the gas at the same time. A bright handle to the far left releases the pedal-type parking brake, which flies off with a thunk. The clutch comes back easily, and we're off. First gear of the optional four-speed is a creeper, and even second is still pretty low for an empty truck, so Leo recommends a third-gear start.

Since this truck doesn't haul much of anything these days Leo has installed 4.11 rear-end gears, for reasonably comfortable 60-mph cruising. With the original 5.14 gears, he said, the truck "could climb a tree" in first but was "screaming" at 50 mph in fourth. (Factory specs claimed a top speed of only 62 mph, at the "maximum recommended" 3,000 rpm—and that was with the standard 4.57 ratio rather than the 5.14 option!) The down-side of this modification is

some loss of low-end flexibility. In stock tune, the GMC mill produces no abundance of torque, and I feel as though I am working a little engine hard to haul around a fairly big truck.

The gearbox is synchronized in second through fourth, although it feels more like a very fine, prewar, non-synchro unit, its long lever snicks cleanly from gear to gear only after I've mastered its rhythm. At very low speed, a careful and deliberate hand can slip it smartly from fourth down to third without double clutching; otherwise a double-pump on the clutch, punctuated by a slight blip on the throttle, eases the downshift that's more or less necessary for any 90 degree turn.

And the driveline is loud. Standing up on the curb, watching Leo pitch the truck around, we heard mostly the arrogant snort of the exhaust—a confident, powerful snarl. Inside the cab, however,

the gearbox howls like a storm through a narrow canyon, drowning out the cheeky exhaust. As you can see, the truck leans quite lot in the turns, but the driver feels more in control than the photos suggest. The stiff suspension enhances stability and confidence in steady-state cornering, so that the pickup seems a bit more secure than a softer-sprung 1949 passenger car. But the steering, while it requires only car-level effort, responds slowly and not always predictably. Try a sharp left-right around a pothole, and the GMC wallows nautically, its loose steering and old-fashioned lever shocks unable to keep pace with its mass—this was the last year for lever shocks. And the stiff suspension responds to every bump in the road. The ride is not harsh or uncomfortable, but it is constantly in motion.

The brakes work well for their time, requiring average effort, while returning slightly above-average modulation and stopping power. Like so much else on this surprising truck, they compare favorably to contemporary passenger-car equipment.

But unbeknownst to many, before there was a Chevrolet truck—almost before there was a Chevrolet car —there was a truck called GMC. In fact, GM's premium truck division could trace its roots back to a chain-drive truck called Rapid, which was first manufactured in Detroit in 1902. Rapid opened a new plant in Pontiac, Michigan, in 1905, and was soon turning out 200 trucks a year. GMC would later claim that this was the world's first factory devoted entirely to commercial-vehicle production.

Rapid was acquired by the newly founded General Motors in 1909, around the same time that GM also bought a Detroit-based truck manufacturer called Reliance. At first, the General planned to sell both Rapid and

ADVANCE-DESIGN ADVANCES

Chevrolet marketed its Advance-Design trucks as 1947½ models. GMC never fussed much over model years, so even though its new trucks appeared at the same time, some sources identify them as '48s. In any case, a model changeover of sorts occurred at the end of that first summer—at least on 100s and 150s—when the gearshift moved from the floor to the steering column and the handbrake was replaced by a pedal, thus clearing out the middle of the floor for a third passenger. The optional heavy-duty four-speed still came with a floor shift.

For '49, GM rounded off the corners of the parking-brake pedal and the in-cab fuel tank became standard after the cab mounts were moved to the side frame rails. 1951 brought vent windows, and push-button door handles appeared for late '52. At GMC, horsepower progressed to 96 in '50 and then 100 in '51,

and Hydra-Matic arrived as an option for '53.

The '54 GMC pickup suffered from a somewhat heavy-handed facelift, but was now powered by the 248-cu.in. Six from the division's medium-duty line. (It was just a 228 with an additional 5/32-inch of bore.) When the all-new '55-1/2 models arrived they were very handsome indeed, featuring crisp and car-like horizontal lines. GMC reverted to its prewar preference for massive grillwork to distinguish itself from Chevrolet, but still arguably built the better-looking truck of the two. Of course Chevy had a new 265-cu.in. V-8, but GMC was able to borrow Pontiac's equally new 287-cu.in. V-8 and maintain its horsepower advantage. The 248-cu.in. Six remained the standard engine until 1963, when for the first time GMC installed a Chevy Six as its base-level power plant.

Easy to access side-mounted spare tire.

Fresh air cab vent very effective when hot.

It's country-style!

GMC
GASOLINE & DIESEL TRUCKS
¾ TO 20 TONS

Get a real truck!

Reliance-brand trucks under the umbrella of the General Motors Truck Company, or GMC for short. But the Rapid and Reliance names both vanished during 1912, and in 1913 the manufacture of all GMC trucks—up to 4,000 per year by then—was consolidated at the former Rapid plant in Pontiac.

In those early years, GMC's light trucks were electrics; only the 1-1/2-ton to 5-ton models were gasoline powered. It wasn't until 1916 that GMC replaced the electric delivery models with 3/4-ton and 1-ton trucks powered by a Continental Four. Many of these served as ambulances during the Great War. GMC began building its own four-cylinder engines during 1920, then dropped the 3/4-ton model for 1923, to focus on trucks of 1-ton capacity and heavier. Meanwhile, Chevrolet entered the truck market in January 1918, with a 1/2-ton based on the Four-Ninety passenger car as well as a heavier, 1-ton model.

GMC returned to light trucks through a somewhat circuitous route. GM's Oakland division introduced its Pontiac passenger car in January 1926, followed by a Pontiac 1/2-ton truck in October. Then corporate management decided to transfer the Pontiac truck to GMC, and it was re-badged accordingly for the 1928 model year.

The Pontiac was already based on a Chevrolet chassis, and under the circumstances it was inevitable that Chevrolet and GMC trucks began to share some sheet metal as well. By 1939 they were virtually twins, the GMC distinguished chiefly by a more massive-appearing grille. Engines, however, remained unique to each division. The Pontiac side-valve Six powered light-

duty GMC's into 1933, when it was phased out in favor of a bigger flathead Six of GMC manufacture. Meanwhile, GMC's big trucks had switched to over-head-valve Buick engines, which GMC built itself after 1930. In '39, GMC's light trucks dropped the flathead for a 228-cu.in. version of the Buick-derived, GMC-manufactured, valve-in-head Six.

Nineteen forty-one brought a longer wheelbase, a more modern look—and a subtle reversal in image. Up to that point, GMC styling had been a little more self-consciously massive, even heavy-handed, compared to the prettier Chevrolet. But now it was the Chevy that had the busy look, with its fussy side louvers, and its upper and lower grille sections running two different directions—while the GMC looked comparatively tidy and restrained.

Then came another war. GMC supplied 600,000 trucks, mostly in the 2-1/2-ton range while Chevrolet built air-craft engines and ammunition.

The first all-new, postwar vehicles from GM, Ford, and Chrysler were not cars but trucks. In The Heavyweight Book of American Light Trucks 1939-1966, authors Tom Brownell and Don Bunn offer as likely an explanation for this as we've seen anywhere. The war had shut down car production more or less completely, whereas the truck lines were kept running, mostly for the mili-

tary but also for critical civilian businesses. So afterward, it was easier to push a new truck into production than a new car.

Dodge introduced its all-new B-1 truck line in December 1947, more than a year before Chrysler would have an all-new passenger car. Ford released a re-styled F-Series truck in January '48; the new Lincolns, Mercurys, and Fords then trickled out behind it. Even Studebaker managed to launch an all-

specifications

1949 GMC FC-152 3/4-ton pickup

125.25 inches

61.8 inches

Base price	$1,390
Std. equipment	Electric horn; oil-wetted air cleaner; single-acting front and rear shocks; spring-mounted, chrome front bumper; spare wheel (without tire); left-side taillight.
Options on dR car	Four-speed transmission, chrome grille, fresh-air-type heater, dual taillights, visor, traffic signal viewer, HD wheels and tires, side-mount spare
Price as equipped	N/A

ENGINE

Type	6 in-line
Bore x stroke	3.5625 inches x 3.8125 inches
Displacement	228 cubic inches
Compression ratio	6.75:1
Horsepower @ rpm	93 @ 3,000
Torque @ rpm	182 @ 1,000-2,000
Taxable horsepower	30.4
Valve gear	Ohv
Valve lifters	Mechanical
Main bearings	4
Induction	1-bbl Zenith
Fuel system	AC mechanical pump
Lubrication system	Pressure, gear-type pump
Cooling system	Pressure, centrifugal pump
Exhaust system	Single
Electrical system	6-volt, D.C., positive ground

TRANSMISSION

Type	4-speed manual, synchronized on 2nd-4th
Ratios	1st: 7.06:1; 2nd: 3.58:1; 3rd: 1.71:1; 4th: 1.00:1; Reverse: 6.78:1

CLUTCH

Type	Single dry plate
Diameter	10.75 inches

REAR AXLE

Drive axle	Rear, hypoid, full-floating
Ratio	Originally 5.14:1; now 4.11:1

STEERING

Type	Recirculating ball
Ratio	26.24:1
Turns lock-to-lock	N/A
Turning circle	N/A

BRAKES

Type	4-wheel hydraulic,
Front	11.0 x 1.75-inch drum
Rear	12.0 x 2.0-inch drum
Swept area	271 square inches
Parking brake	Mechanical, on rear drums

CHASSIS & BODY

Construction	Channel-section ladder frame with 5 crossmembers, separate body
Body style	2-door, 3-seat pickup truck

SUSPENSION

Front	Forged I-beam axle, semi-elliptic leaf springs
Rear	Live axle, semi-elliptic leaf springs

Shock absorbers	Front: hydraulic, lever-type Rear: hydraulic, lever-type
Tires	Michelin X 8R17.5
Wheels	2-piece pressed steel, 17.5 in.

WEIGHTS AND MEASURES

Wheelbase	125.25 inches
Overall length	200.25 inches
Overall width	70.2 inches
Overall height	N/A inches
Front track	61.8 inches
Rear track	61.8 inches
Min. road clearance	9 inches
Curb weight	3,595 pounds
GVW	5,800 pounds

CAPACITIES

Crankcase	9.5 quarts (w/filter)
Transmission	6 quarts
Cooling system	18 quarts
Fuel tank	18 gallons
Drive axle	6 pints

CALCULATED DATA

Bhp/c.i.d.	0.41
Stroke/bore	1.07
Lb./bhp	38.6
Lb. per sq. in. (brakes)	13.3

Optional windshield visor aided driver's vision and kept cab cooler.

new truck for '49, although by then South Bend had debuted an all-new (and strikingly modern) automobile.

General Motors beat them all to market with its Advance-Design series in June 1947.

The corporation had interviewed truck owners nationwide to find out what they wanted, and what they wanted was more: more room, more comfort, improved visibility and ventilation—and better styling. Business owners recognized that the look of their trucks helped shape their public image. The Advance-Design trucks were certainly clean-lined and modern, with alligator

Distinguished chrome grille was optional.

Elegant-looking GMC logo adorned the straight-six's valve cover.

hoods and headlights fully integrated into their fenders. Bumpers were larger, and a gravel guard filled the space between the bumper and the grille. The fenders could be painted body color, instead of black as before, and a chrome grille was an option. Even the parking lights glowed 50 percent brighter.

The windshield was wider, taller, and raked back further. The door windows and backlight were larger as well, providing nearly 15 percent more glass area in the standard cab. Optional "deluxe" cabs came with bright trim around the windshield and door glass, plus curved rear quarter windows that boosted the total glass area to 40 percent more than on the '46 models.

The windshield no longer swung open at the bottom; this allowed GM to relocate the wipers for a more effective sweep, but it also cut off an important source of fresh air. That's probably why the General made the cowl-top ventilator larger and sturdier, and gave it a bug screen for the first time—while adding the second ventilator to the driver's side footwell. The heater intake on the right side, combined with outlets in the floor behind the seat, provided an early sort of passive, flow-through ventilation.

But most importantly, Advance-Design cabs were larger all around. Passengers gained 8 inches of hip room, and another 3-1/2 inches of shoulder-level width. Foot space was a huge 12 inches wider. The tubular-framed seat contained nearly twice as many springs, and the springs were individually wrapped—more like the construction of a passenger-car seat. The seat could be ordered with genuine leather upholstery. Door handles and window winders worked more smoothly, and pedals were re-positioned for more comfortable operation. Steering required less muscle, thanks to a larger wheel and revised linkage geometry.

Advance-Design chassis were all new as well, with longer springs for a better ride, and re-engineered transmissions, including an-all new, helical-gear, synchromesh four-speed rated for up to 16,000 pounds GVW. Trucks rated 3/4 ton (like the driveReport truck) or heavier differed significantly in chassis design from the lighter half tons, having

open propeller shafts and Hotchkiss drive, compared to the half-ton's torque-tube. Three-quarter-ton models also featured deeper-section frames stamped from thicker steel, full-floating axles, and two-stage springs front and rear. Their clutch measured 10-3/4 inches in diameter rather than the 1/2-ton's 9-1/2 (Chevy) or 9 (GMC).

GMC offered its 1/2-ton with either a 116-inch-wheelbase and 78-inch bed (Model FC-101) or a 125.25-inch wheelbase and 87-inch bed (FC-102). The 3/4-ton FC-152 came only with the longer wheelbase and bed, while the 1-ton FC-253 rode on a 137-inch wheelbase and carried a 108-inch bed. Height and width of all three beds were standardized at 16-1/4 inches and 50 inches, respectively, to simplify production, and all three were lined with long-leaf yellow pine. Various other capacity/wheelbase combinations were offered as chassis or chassis-and-cab-only for custom bodies. Hood badges were simplified to "100," "150," or "250" regardless of wheelbase or body style.

GM's heavy trucks were all new too, and shared the Advance-Design cab. Their larger size required different sheet metal ahead of the cowl, but basically

ON THE MARKET

While light-duty Chevrolet trucks are a dime a dozen, 3/4-ton GMCs are difficult to find. Browsing www.hemmings.com and back issues of *Hemmings Motor News*, we discovered three trucks for sale. Although some need a full restoration and one is supposedly restored but "needs work," overall, 3/4-ton GMC trucks are rather affordable.

1949 GMC 3/4-ton pickup, rust-free Texas truck with straight body, runs, but needs work. $2,600.

1949 GMC 3/4-ton pickup truck, runs good, needs full restoration. $500.

1949 GMC 3/4-ton pickup, 6-cyl, 4-spd, older restoration, needs some TLC. $4,500.

PARTS PRICES

Stainless Steel headlight bezel	$20
Carburetor rebuild kit	$30
Driveshaft rebuild kit	$40
Brake shoes (front)	$50
Door weatherstripping	$105
Complete engine gasket set	$120
Brake line set	$145
Seat upholstery kit	$155
Front bumper	$230
Wooden planks for bed floor	$800

POWER GAMES

The 93-hp that we've quoted for the GMC 228-cu.in. Six is the number seen most often; it represents gross output at the "maximum recommended engine speed" of 3,000 rpm and is, we believe, the fairest number to use when comparing the GMC's performance to the contemporary Chevrolet's 90-hp maximum gross" bhp of 94.5 at 3,200 rpm, and a net output of 85.5 bhp at 3,000.

To make matters more confusing, GMC attributed all these numbers to the "Super Duty 228" which, as far was we can tell, was actually the standard-equipment engine. Buyers opting for the "Standard Engine" got a modified intake manifold that sacrificed performance for fuel economy. A third variation, the "Special Economy Engine," had yet another restricted manifold and a higher-compression head.

Solid I-beam front axle is extremely durable but, when rounding tight corners at speed, body roll is a little on the excessive side.

they looked like a scaled-up version of the light truck. Chevrolet called this "Load-Proportioned" styling. It's not clear if GMC used the same term, although its trucks of course followed the same pattern.

One of the few things that hadn't changed with the advent of Advance-Design was motive power—and this is what really set the GMC apart from Chevrolet. GMC's 228 rated 93-hp and 182-lb.ft. of torque, compared to 90 and 174, respectively, for the 216-cu.in. Chevy. Both engines were overhead-

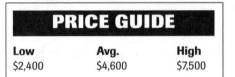

PRICE GUIDE

Low	Avg.	High
$2,400	$4,600	$7,500

valve sixes with four-bearing cranks, but the GMC was fully pressure-lubed, while the Chevy's rod bearings still depended on the dip-and-splash method at low rpm. GMC pistons were aluminum, not cast iron, and their floating pins were pressure-lubed through

rifle-drilled con rods. And the GMC camshaft was driven by helical-cut gears of steel (on the crank) and aluminum (on the cam), rather than the fiber gears that Chevrolet used.

Other small details separated the GMC from the Chevrolet and helped justify its slightly higher price. For example, the GMC had an 18-quart cooling system to Chevrolet's 15. The 1/2-ton long-bed variant appears to have been a GMC exclusive, as Chevrolet sources simply don't mention it. GMC frames were heavier in construction, and

OR YOU COULD BUY...
The 1949 3/4-Tons Compared

	Studebaker 2R10	Dodge B-1-C	Chevrolet 3600	GMC FC-152	International KB-2	Ford F-2
Price	$1,367	$1,371	$1,372	$1,390	$1,399	$1,466
Cylinders	6	6	6	6	6	6
Bore x Stroke	3.0 x 4.0	3.25 x 3.62	3.5 x 3.75	3.56 x 3.81	3.31 x 4.12	3.3 x 3.4
C.I.D.	170	218	216	228	213	226
Compression	6.5:1	6.6:1	6.6:1	6.75:1	6.3:1	6.8:1
Valve gear	L-head	L-head	OHV	OHV	L-head	Valve gear L-head
Bhp @ rpm	80 @ 4,000	95 @ 3,600	90 @ 3,300	93 @ 3,000	82 @ 3,400	95 @ 3,300
Wheelbase (in.)	112	116	125.25	125.25	125	122
Box length(in.)	78	90	87	87	na	96
Tires	6.00 x 16	7.00 x 15	7.50 x 15	7.50 x 15	7.00 x 16	7.50 x 16
Weight (lb.)	3,040	3,525	3,520	3,595	3,020	3,555
Stroke/bore	1.33	1.11	1.07	1.07	1.24	1.03
Bhp/C.I.D.	0.47	0.44	0.42	0.41	0.38	0.42
Lb./Bhp	38.0	37.1	39.1	38.6	36.8	37.4

reached out one more inch ahead of the front wheels to accommodate the slightly bulkier engine. And while the difference in appearance between the two brands was subtle, it required different grilles, engine hoods, and fenders—although the sheet metal parts were similar enough that they probably could have shared some tooling.

None of which is surprising, because GMC operated as much as a semi-independent entity within General Motors as any of the car-building divisions. In 1949, the year our driveReport truck was produced, GMC employed 700 engineers, maintained its own staff of 30 at the Proving Grounds, and cataloged eight unique gasoline-powered engines (plus two unique diesels). Its four factories covered a total of 5 million square feet on a 600-acre site in Pontiac. One and a half million square feet, including an extensive new engine lab, had been added since the end of the war. ◐

CLUB SCENE

National Chevy/GMC Truck Association
P.O. Box 607458
Dept. SIA-179
Orlando, FL 32860
407-889-5549
E-mail: chevy55-72@ao.net
Dues: $30/year; Members: 1,800

Stylish round gauges have chrome bezels.

Expansive dashboard is all painted metal.

Turn signals are a much needed option.

DREAM TRUCK

Most special-interest enthusiasts will work hard and sacrifice much to own the vehicle of their dreams. But we think Leo Ethier worked harder and sacrificed more than most to acquire his Advance-Design GMC. "I looked for it for 35 years, almost," he told us. "I started working in a body shop when I was 14, and the guy who owned the shop had a GMC wrecker, an old deuce-and-a-half from the army. I'd look at it every day through the window, and say to myself, 'I could really turn that old sum-bitch into something if I had the opportunity.' " Later on, Leo managed a number of body shops, but never found time to restore a vehicle of his own.

He finally opened his own shop in Riverside, N.J., in 1995, and went looking for a GMC pickup like the one he had admired so long ago. He soon found the driveReport truck in a yard in Palmyra, "all hanging down and rusted into the ground."

It had been delivered new in Kansas, put into storage when it was just a year old, and then taken out in 1976 and put to work in a coal yard. Then the owner commissioned a painting (not of the truck, we presume) and didn't pay for it; the artist acquired the truck in the settlement, parked it in his yard, and let it deteriorate. The odometer showed only 6,000 miles, but Leo is certain the truck must have covered 106,000, or maybe even 206,000. "I finally convinced him to sell it to me," Leo continued.

"At the time I didn't have any money, because I had just opened my shop. So I sold my El Camino - the only vehicle I owned - and walked to work for a year, to earn this truck. I worked on it every night for six months." He painted it, in its original two-tone colors, during the blizzard of '96, then had to literally dig his way home with a snow shovel. His employees complained about the shop space that the truck occupied. Leo replied that when the truck was finished, it would bring priceless publicity for the business.

And it has. Leo's GMC won DuPont's Top Gun award in 1996 and has won more than 100 other awards, including best 1947-54 truck at the

Carlisle All-Truck Nationals. It regularly tops modified trucks at hot-rod shows. It has even appeared on the Mother's Car Show Series on ESPN2. The series was covering a Super Chevy show at Maple Grove Raceway in Reading, Pennsylvania, where Leo's truck caught the eye of co-host Don Garlits. Garlits recalled how the 228-cu.in. GMC Six was a favorite of drag racers back in 1949-51, when its more sophisticated oiling system allowed it to be tuned for more horsepower than a Chevrolet Six - or, for that matter, a 221-cu.in. flathead Ford. Garlits then pronounced the truck worth $30,000. Leo drove home with the first-place trophy in the 1949-72 category, once again out-gunning the hot rods.

In AACA competition, however, the highest Leo's truck has ever scored is a third Junior, and Leo readily admits that the judges have disputed some details of his restoration. Most critical are the wheels and tires. GMC sales literature listed five different tire options for the 3/4-ton truck, ranging from a standard six-ply, 15-inch tire up to an eight-ply 7.50 x 17. One-ton models were officially offered with 7.00 x 17, 7.50 x 17, or 7.00 x 18 rubber. But Leo found his truck riding on 8.00 x 17.5's, with a spare and rim the same size. According to the previous owner, the spare was the original; it had certainly been there a long time, as it had literally rotted into the rim and had to be cut off. Rob English, a GMC part supplier himself, and technical advisor for the National Chevy/GMC Truck Association, told us that other GMC's from this era

have shown up with 17.5-inch wheels as well—although most of them have been one-tons. In any case, the only tires currently available in this somewhat unusual size are Michelin X radials - clearly not authentic, but they don't hurt the truck's ride any.

The engine color has also been questioned, but Leo told us he'd "looked at 17 GMC engines in junk yards, and every one was gloss black." Rob also believes that black is the correct color. The truck already had a four-speed gearbox, fresh-air heater, and an overhead-signal prism when Leo found it. He added the factory-optional right side tail light himself, along with a side-mounted spare and an aftermarket sun visor. He said that he'd like to install a radio, if only because it would make the interior look a little more finished. Without one, there's a blanking plate on the dash, and wiring shows through the open speaker grille. But that's the way the factory made them.

As nice as his truck is, Leo doesn't hesitate to drive it, and has in fact put 10,000 miles on it in the last two years. "We do a show every weekend," he said. "I try to get as much publicity as I can for my shop."

What should collectors look for when buying an Advance-Design GMC? Leo grinned at the question. This is where most owners advise us to watch out for hidden rust, or to pass on any example that doesn't have all its trim. But Leo believes these trucks are too rare for that. "Good luck finding one," he answered, "and if you do, grab it, because you're not going to find another one." Parts, on the other hand, are less of a problem than you might think, particularly the pieces that were shared by Chevrolet.

Leo spoke highly of all of the suppliers on the list below. (We added the National Chevy/GMC Truck Association, plus Rob English's parts business and of course Leo's own shop, which did the bodywork and coordinated the entire restoration.) Mostly, however, Leo asked us to thank Bob Grab and son, all the friends who helped with the restoration, and especially his wife, Willy.

Historic Hauler
Hudson's Car-like 1946 Cab Pickup Truck

By John F. Katz

Photography by the Vince Wright

Hudson badge integrated into grille.

Teardrop headlamp bezels and elaborate grille give Hudson an upscale look.

Hustling through the park for flash-by photos, I heard a loud hum and saw the dark, low shape in my mirror. He was clearly in a bigger hurry, so I pulled right and let him pass: a gleaming Accord coupe, seriously slammed, with windows as black as the paintwork and mirrored panels pasted on the lower body. I didn't expect to see it again.

But there it was, when I pulled into the parking area to turn around—squatting about three inches off the pavement, on wide 40-profile rubber that was barely contained by his bolt-on fender flairs. A buzz-cut kid in baggy pants was meticulously detailing the trunk. He looked up at

the Hudson truck—what would he think of this?—and a broad smile split his sun-burned face. Then he waved.

It was a real Verizon-ad moment: You know, where the hip young kid smiles at the old geezer 'cause they're on the same calling plan? A heartwarming brother-hood of motorheads, and maybe it was. But then I wondered if my new Genera-tion-Y friend thought that this box-stock Hudson was custom. Just like his Honda.

A Hudson pickup certainly looks cus-tom. With its passenger-car front end mated to its wide, utilitarian truck box, it looks for all the world like something that wasn't meant to be, like something Willy welded up out behind the service station. This isn't entirely an illusion. Pickups rep-resented a microscopic percentage of Hudson production, and building them involved a certain amount of hand-fabri-cation, using modified sheet metal from a four-door sedan. Fit and finish were first-rate, mind you, but the very concept sug-gests something homemade.

Not only does a Hudson pickup look like the front half of a car, it drives like one too. It may be, in fact, the most car-like truck I've ever driven, handling more like an average sedan of its own time than even today's more technically sophisticat-ed, but relatively gargantuan, full-size pickups handle like a Camry or a Taurus.

The oil-soaked cork clutch does require a lot of motion, as if you were stepping over something; it would be wearying in traffic. The column shifter squeezes tight-ly into first with a slight groan of com-plaint, and then that wet clutch comes back with a shudder. Then the deep, chug-ging idle of that long-stroke six gives way to a liquid, busy howl—like the sound of most American sixes, less a rhythm than a

whir. The Hudson hits 25 mph in a heart-beat, and the shift lever slides more easily into second. Forty seems plenty fast in intermediate gear, but I think the engine would have kept right on pulling had I not up-shifted into high. The Hudson almost seems to enjoy hard use, its shifter moving easier, not harder, the faster I rev the en-gine between shifts. Down-shifts come easily enough, as long as I remember to hesitate for three beats in neutral. Accelera-tion is satisfyingly quick, subjectively as good as in any six-cylinder sedan in those times, and maybe even nipping the heels of some eights.

Even the steering feels direct and tight, with enough road feel to inspire confi-dence, and reasonable enough effort as long as the truck is rolling. Tossed into a 40mph turn, the Hudson heels over and plows as dramatically as any mid-Forties sedan—but no more so—and even the outside front tire doesn't complain until I try it again at 45 mph. The ride is firm and controlled, but smothers bumps effective-ly; the brakes are easily modulated, and remained free from fade despite repeated hard stops for our action photography ses-sion.

Like I said: As trucks go, the Hudson's a pretty good handling car.

Historic Hudson Haulers

Hudson built light-duty trucks under a variety of names, beginning with the Essex-derived Dover of 1929. Documen-tation on these vehicles is very thin, and they do not appear to have been very suc-cessful. A line of nearly identical trucks (leftovers, perhaps?) were sold with Essex badges through 1932, when they were re-placed by a new range of pickups and deliveries based on Terraplane mechani-cals. These may have debuted under the Essex name but were sold as Terraplanes in 1934–38. Sales peaked in '37 at 8,058 units.

From 1937, Hudson itself offered a line of "Commercial Cars," including a sedan delivery, a station wagon, and a cab-and-chassis. Also offered was a "Utility Coupe," with a small pickup box that pulled out from the trunk like a drawer; and a "Utility Coach," a two-door sedan from which all seats save the driver's could be removed. Blind side panels installed over the rear quarter windows.

The "Commercial Cars" became "Busi-ness Cars" in 1938, the same year that the Terraplane became the Hudson Terra-plane and then flew off into the sunset. For 1939, however, Hudson fielded its widest range of commercials yet, in sever-al trim levels and on at least three different wheelbases. Among these was a stylish

Distinct hood ornament design similar to that used on later Hornets and Wasp models.

The front end shared a lot of sheet metal with the Super Six four-door sedan, yet most of the cab was fabricated by hand.

panel truck with Hudson Pacemaker-level trim, bodied by Checker, of Kalamazoo.

Topping them all, however, was the new, 3/4-ton "Big Boy" heavy-duty commercial line. This consisted of a pickup and a sedan delivery, plus five and seven-passenger sedans—presumably for the taxi and limo trade—all sharing passenger-car styling, on a 119-inch wheelbase and powered by a 212-cu.in. straight-six. Yet despite this variety of choices, only 640 commercial Hudsons were shipped that year.

A handsome new front end graced Hudson cars and trucks for 1940, along with a proper double-wishbone and coil-spring front suspension. (Hudson had offered the leaf-sprung Baker Axle-Flex system as an option in '34–'35, then reverted to a beam axle on leaf springs, guided by radius rods, through '39.) On the Big Boys, a longer, 125-inch wheelbase enhanced the new look. The line now included a "seven-passenger carry-all," which was a heavy-duty sedan with seats that folded to make room for cargo. Still, commercial production bobbed up only listlessly, to 1,035. That Hudson persisted in spite of such low numbers strongly suggests that management never expected to sell many more that.

Hudson bodies were new and more modern-looking for 1941. The Big Boy chassis was stretched to its definitive 128 inches, the same as a flagship Commodore Eight sedan. War production brought profits, welcome after Depression losses even in 1940. Like everyone else's, Hudson's 1942 passenger cars were a bit flashier, with new front and rear fenders and trim that suggested a full-width grille. The lower body flared out to conceal the running boards. Consumer production was suspended on February 5, 1942.

Hudson resumed automobile production on August 30, 1945. The passenger cars looked a lot like the '42s, except for an elaborate grille that faded inward in the middle. The grille has been credited to Art Kibiger, and is significant for a couple of

THREE-QUARTER TONS OF REALITY

When I drove a '49 GMC 3/4-ton pickup for *SIA* #179, what impressed me most was its heavy-duty seriousness. The Hudson is equally impressive, but for its car-like styling and comfort. Both were rated 3/4-ton by their manufacturer. Yet the Hudson is far more lightly sprung and more steeply geared, suggesting a 1946 El Camino more than a serious hauler. Could it possibly carry as much as the GMC, or hold up as well under years of hard use?

The answer, in all probability, is no. We consulted with Kit Foster, who writes SIA's "Lost and Found," and who has extensively researched the Hudson pickups. As Kit noted, subtracting the Hudson's shipping weight from its GVW (see specification chart) leaves 1,700 pounds, which looks like a generous 3/4 ton—until you subtract from that the weight of a driver and a tank of gas. Then the Hudson still hauls its advertised capacity, but just barely.

Applying the same math to the '46 Hudson's 3/4-ton competitors yields much higher actual load capacities: 2,360 pounds for a Chevrolet 3600, 2,215 for a GMC FC-152, 1,975 for a Dodge WD-15 and a whopping 2,952 for the Ford 79Y, which Dearborn, still with some modesty, billed as a one-ton. "It's not that Hudson was hyperventilating," Kit commented. "It's that the Big Three were more conservative in rating their trucks.

"To an extent, they still are. I've owned a number of contemporary so-called 3/4-ton pickups, both Chevrolet and Dodge, and they have tended to weigh just under 5,000 pounds. But they've had GVW's of 7,500–9,000 pounds. I used them regularly to fetch 3,000 pounds of loose coal."

Whereas, when Hudson said 3/4 ton, Hudson meant 1,499 pounds—and not an ounce more.

> *"A handsome new front end graced Hudson cars and trucks for 1940, along with a proper double-wishbone and coil-spring front suspension."*

Deco-styled lettering same as that used on the entry-level Super Six on which it is based.

reasons. For one, it was die-cast, where previous Hudson grilles had been stamped. For another, it used a painted black background—an industry first, but one that would not become widely popular for almost another 20 years. The new front end was supposed to visually add mass and subtract height, which it probably did, although the 1940–41 look had been arguably much cleaner.

A simplified model lineup offered just two trim levels, both on a 121-inch wheelbase: the very nice Super and the even more deluxe Commodore. Either could be ordered with a 102hp, 212-cu.in. straight-six or a 128hp, 254-cu.in. straight-eight. The Commodore Eight benefited from a bigger clutch, radiator and brakes plus lower-profile 15-inch wheels.

Secrets revealed

The first Hudsons to roll down off the revived assembly line were Super Six sedans, and 3/4-ton pickups soon followed. But all of the smaller trucks were forgotten and, without them for comparison, the Big Boy name seems to have been dropped as well. Hudson's sole commercial vehicle was now called simply the Cab Pickup.

Its sheet metal had been frozen in 1941; the pickup never would see the '42 passenger cars' new fenders and concealed running boards. Hudson did dress it up with the post-war grille and dashboard, which by themselves updated its look fairly effectively. Mechanically, it was based on the entry-level Super Six, and clearly shared some sheet metal and tooling with the '41 Super Six four-door sedan. The doors were identical. A lot of the cab appears to have been hand-fabricated using modified pre-war four-door panels and tooling.

"When we stripped the body," noted Dave Brady, owner of our driveReport truck, "we could see where they had done that." Hudson used similar methods for building low-production convertibles, using modified coupe panels.

The post-war pickup retained its now-unique 128-inch wheelbase; it rode on stiffer springs than the Super Six sedan, and borrowed its 11-inch brake drums

Exterior spotlights fitted on both sides.

Exhaust tip emblazoned with logo.

ADVENTURES IN LIGHT-DUTY TRUCKING

Dave Brady acquired his Hudson pickup as an advertising vehicle for his business, Dave's Interior Restorations, in Emmaus, Pennsylvania. "I have a '51 Chevrolet sedan-delivery already," he told us. "But one of my customers, who owned a Hudson, said that if I wanted something really unusual I should get a Hudson truck. So I started looking around, and I found this one in April 1998."

As far as Dave can tell, his truck was sold originally in Kansas, and went through at least four owners there before spending two decades with a single owner in Indiana. Then it went to northern Michigan, where it was superficially restored as a fire chief's truck.

The "chief" misrepresented the truck somewhat, telling Dave that it was an award-winner that was never driven, but always trailered. "Well," Dave noted, "the reason it was always trailered was because it was undriveable, and the only award it had won was because it was the only vehicle in its class." The condition of the truck brought new meaning to the term "cosmetic restoration": The switch for the non-functioning windshield wipers had been glued to the dashboard.

Dave decided to restore the truck as a run-ner, and with every conceivable accessory. Everything you see on the driveReport truck was available through Hudson dealers—except for the rear fender skirts, which are an authentic aftermarket item. We doubt that many owners prettied up their trucks quite so much when they were new, but the accessories certainly contribute to the impression of a customized vehicle.

Before he installed all the accessories, of course, Dave tore the truck down to its bare frame. He sent the engine to Hedley Bennett in London, Ontario. The odometer showed only 58,000 miles, "but the engine builder said it had to be 258,000. Everything, literally everything, was worn out." Dave bought an overdrive transmission from, and had the rear-end re-built by, Al Saffrahn in Maricopa, Arizona.

"The rest we handled here in my own shop." The bed was mostly bondo and had to be reproduced, but the remainder of the original body panels were all good enough to save. Dave had D. Duncan Autos, of Allentown, paint the finished truck Bar Harbor Blue, an authentic and attractive hue for the breed.

With its rare aftermarket fender skirts fitted to the flowing fenders, the Hudson pickup has a dramatic, yet elegant, appearance about it.

from the Hudson Eight, replacing the 10-inch units Hudson supplied with six-cylinder passenger cars. Because of the super-duty leaves in the rear, rear shock absorbers were optional. But most other part numbers would exchange with those of a Super Six passenger car.

Having the cab section of a passenger car meant that the Hudson pickup shared the car's column-mounted gearshift and independent front suspension. No other domestic pickup would have a column shifter before 1949, and independent suspensions would not arrive until the 1960s. (Recall that Ford and Lincoln-Mercury passenger cars not have independent front suspension until 1949.) The Hudson truck also shared the passenger car's brightly trimmed dashboard and offered its 30-hour clock, Zenith radio, Weather-Master heater, and deluxe steering wheel with chrome horn ring as options.

Tilt the enormous hood forward, and some of the secrets of the Hudson's handling are revealed. The independent front end is immediately apparent, with its huge lower wishbones reaching almost to the centerline of the vehicle. But even more important, I suspect, is the location of the engine. The little flathead straight-six fits almost entirely behind the front-wheel centerline. So the Hudson pickup is as much a mid-engine machine as today's quarter-million-dollar, desert-racing Trophy Trucks. The Hudson even has its tall, tall radiator snugged back close to its engine, with an enormous sheet-metal pan channeling cooling air from the grille.

The bed is enormous. It measures 93 x 57 x 18-5/16 inches, with 48-3/8 inches between the inside fender wells, making it nearly as large as today's full-size eight-footers. It is so wide that its sides intersect the wheel wells. This leaves part of the wheelwell on the inside of the bed, as in a modern "wideside" pickup. But then part of the wheelwell also remains outside of the bed, as on a traditional step-side or

Compared to other pickups, entry into the cabin is easy, due to the cab's low stance.

"Despite the Hudson's rich styling and impressive length, the cab still feels claustrophobic."

"sportside." So while the Hudson may not possess the earliest-known full-width bed, it may well represent an important and largely unheralded step in that direction.

Up until only a few years ago, pickups tended to be fairly stark inside. But recall that the Hudson pickup borrowed the elaborately styled dashboard of the Super Six sedan. Instrument markings are all on the surface of the panel, with indicator needles moving in windows behind them—unnecessarily intricate, but still legible. The only actual gauges are for speed, fuel level, and water temperature. A pair of idiot lights are located way over on the passenger side, just above the glove box; when activated, the word "NO" appears in a red square over the permanently inscribed "OIL" or "GEN" on the dashboard. Cute.

The knob at the end of the shifter is ivory colored and shaped like an egg, or maybe an old-fashioned outdoor Christmas bulb. Similar ivory-colored ovoids terminate the turn-signal lever and hood release.

A bright, inset speaker grille surrounds the radio at the center of the dash. All of the accessory controls feel tight, almost stiff. The starter is a big, square button at the bottom edge of the panel. The handbrake is a chrome handle, under the dash at the extreme left. The heater controls hang under the dash, toward the right; I wouldn't want to have to fiddle with them while I was moving.

On the positive side, the Hudson has one of the safer-looking dashboards I've seen from this era. The steering wheel hub is broad and flat, like a mid-'60s Mercedes. Nothing is padded, of course, but nothing sticks out threateningly, either.

Yet, despite the Hudson's rich styling and impressive length, the cab still feels claustrophobic, with just barely enough space between the dashboard and the back wall. Head room is generous, but leg room is just adequate for a six-footer. The side windows, although shared with the Hudson sedan, seem like small, round portholes on the pickup, conspiring with the tank-slit windshield and tiny round backlight to create blind spots. The seat itself is as flat, hard, and unnaturally

Carter single-barrel downdraft feeds fuel to the 102hp, 212-cu.in. L-head in-line six.

Hudson made it all, including its bodies.

Tailgate hardware is simple, yet effective.

upright as the proverbial park bench, but that seems to bother me more than it does Dave. "You can drive all day in this truck," he smiled, threading through the

alleyways behind his shop. "We drove to Nashville with just 40 miles on the restoration. And when you get out, you don't feel achy or tired, because you're sitting in the

Big wheel needed to make the 18.2:1 ratio manual steering box more manageable.

position you're supposed to be sitting in."

Although the panel delivery was gone, Hudson did offer a "caravan cover" for the pickup, with an aluminum frame and water-resistant "duck" fabric. It attached to the box with just six bolts. Nineteen forty-seven models can be distinguished from '46s by an extra ridge of chrome surrounding the badge above the grille, and by external locks for both doors.

Various sources quote a wide range of prices for the 1946–47 Hudson trucks, from as low as $1,154 to a high of $1,522, a significant 75 percent increase; we can only assume that post-war inflation rapid-

Using adhesive-backed sticker in lieu of rivets, Hudson's tag reads in both English and Spanish.

ly drove the price up. Still, these were essentially good times for Hudson, the last good times it would ever see as an independent manufacturer. Despite dramatic supply shortages, Hudson turned a modest profit of $673,248 in 1945. The company's other blessings included 3,003 dealers nationwide (many with unfilled orders), a thriving overseas business (In Sweden, King Gustav and Crown Prince Olaf both purchased new Hudsons in '45; and the Queen of the Netherlands was a major shareholder), and a product that was widely respected, particularly for ride, handling ease, and solid quality. Hudson

very actively trained returning veterans, and developed special controls for amputees. A five-week strike shut down production in March and April of '46, but Hudson still closed the year with a $2.7 million profit. Hudson would finish calendar-year 1947 with a $5.8 million profit on more than 100,000 vehicles produced. Still, that was only 13th in the industry. Chrysler and Mercury divisions, traditionally behind Hudson, had pulled ahead; so had newcomers Kaiser and Frazer.

Despite dramatically improved sales— 270 in 1945; 3,104 in '46; and 2,917 in '47— Hudson discontinued its pickup line for '48. The usual reason given is that the semi-unitary construction of the '48 "Stepdown" Hudson would not have lent itself to pickup conversion. Yet the factory did build at least one successful '48 prototype, and private individuals created conversions of their own. But compare the 3,104 trucks Hudson built in 1946 against 90,000 Super and Commodore passenger cars, and you see that trucks could not possibly have been a Hudson priority. The pickup may well have been dropped so that the factory could focus on filling the enormous initial demand for Step-down passenger cars.

In its 48-year history, Hudson produced some 30,000 commercial vehicles—about one month's output at Chevrolet in the 1940s.

We wonder if Hudson had built the sharp-looking pickups primarily as advertising vehicles for its dealers. The pickup did perform at least one interesting diplomatic role for Hudson during the all-too-common supply shortages of the early post-war years. Every morning, a squadron of factory-owned pickups would fan out from Detroit in a 100-mile radius, scouring hardware stores for fasteners and other supplies needed on the Hudson assembly line.

But if the Hudson was intended as a kind of boutique pickup, its advertising certainly didn't suggest it. The post-war brochure proudly announced that "a smart, husky new carrier is ready for you!" And yet, the brochure coyly avoided quoting an actual payload capacity or GVW. And an inner paragraph revealed that, "For fast, low-cost delivery service, you can't beat this new, improved Hudson Cab Pick-Up! Smart in appearance and rugged in construction, it is the kind of carrier that will deliver your goods in style . . . ." ᴖ

Wide pleated bench seat is firm and upright.

Rear fenders bolt directly to bed side wall.

Unique radio located in center of dashboard.

Stylish 100-mph speedo is finely crafted.

SPECIFICATIONS: 1946 HUDSON CAB PICKUP

Base price..................................$1,154
Standard equipment includes............Twin windshield wipers, locks for doors and package compartment, cowl vent with screen and water separator, electric horn
Options on dR car..................................Overdrive, rear shock absorbers, "custom" 18-inch steering wheel with horn ring, 30-hour clock, dual spotlights, Weather-Master heater, radio, front bumper guards, fog lights, turn signals, right side arm rest and sun visor, compass, full wheel covers, bumper guards, aftermarket fender skirts

ENGINE
Type..................................Inline 6
Bore x stroke..................................3.0 x 5.0 inches
Displacement..................................212 cubic inches
Compression ratio..................................6.5:1
Bhp (SAE net) @ rpm..................................102 @ 4,000
Torque @ rpm..................................168 lb.ft. @ 1,200
Taxable hp..................................21.6
Valve gear..................................L-head
Fuel delivery..................................Carter 2v downdraft carburetor
Fuel system..................................Mechanical pump
Lubrication system..................................Splash
Exhaust system..................................Single
Electrical system..................................6-volt

CLUTCH
Type..................................Oil-bath, cork-faced
Diameter..................................10 inches
Transmission..................................Three-speed manual plus overdrive
Ratios: 1st..................................2.88:1
2nd..................................1.82:1
3rd..................................1.00:1
Overdrive..................................0.72:1
Reverse..................................3.50:1

DRIVE AXLE
Type..................................Rear, semi-floating
Gear type..................................Spiral-bevel
Ratio..................................4.56:1

STEERING
Type..................................Gemmer worm and roller with centerpoint linkage
Turns, lock-to-lock..................................4.5
Ratio, gear..................................18.2:1
Turning circle, curb-to-curb..................................N/A

BRAKES
Type..................................Bendix, 4-wheel hydraulic with redundant mechanical linkage
Front..................................11 x 1.75-inch drum
Rear..................................11 x 1.75-inch drum
Swept area..................................141 square inches
Construction..................................Ladder frame with box-section side rails, four crossmembers and center x-brace. Separate steel body
Body style..................................3-passenger pickup truck

SUSPENSION
Front..................................Independent, upper and lower A-arms, coil springs, anti-roll bar
Rear..................................Live axle on parallel leaf springs
Shock absorbers..................................Direct-acting hydraulic
Wheels..................................Stamped steel disc, 16 x 4.5
Tires..................................16 x 6.50, 6-ply

WEIGHTS AND MEASURES
Wheelbase..................................128 inches
Front track..................................56.3 inches
Rear track..................................59.5 inches
Overall length..................................216.5 inches
Overall width..................................72.8 inches
Overall height..................................67.8 inches
Minimum ground clearance..................................N/A
Shipping weight..................................3,110 lb.
GVW..................................4,810 lb.

CAPACITIES
Crankcase (refill)..................................4.5 quarts
Fuel tank..................................16.5 gallons
Cooling system..................................13 quarts

CALCULATED DATA
Bhp/c.i.d...................................0.481
Stroke/bore..................................1.667
Lb./bhp..................................30.5
Lb./sq. in. (brakes)..................................22.1

Mighty Mack

The little big pickup that could—Mack's 1937 Jr.

By Dennis David
Photography by the author

When we think of big trucks, the name Mack immediately comes to mind. As one of the premier builders of heavy-duty vehicles, Mack has ties going back to the very beginning of the trucking industry. The company has built trucks that have carried logs across the great timber forests, hauled dirt and gravel to build the nation's dams and highways, and hauled goods from New York to California and all points in between. While it may be easy to stereotype Mack as a builder of nothing but large trucks, there was a time when the company that built "the big ones" offered a small truck. While it certainly couldn't haul heavy loads like its big brothers, the Mack Jr. was well suited to the needs of any small business. Exemplifying all of the styling characteristics of the classic 1930s, the Mack Jr. was a cute pickup truck that was more than capable of earning its keep around the farm, and then taking the family down to the general store.

The roots of the Mack Truck Company can be traced to the five Mack brothers, who began experimenting with self-pro-

more than an extended touring car, it carried one characteristic that would become the hallmark of the Mack name: quality. Evident in every aspect in that very first Mack was a quality of construction not found in many other vehicles of the day. Riding on massive, 36-inch diameter wheels with 4-inch rubber tires and axles constructed of high-grade nickel steel, the Mack brothers' vehicle was built to last. The bus had an incredible carrying capacity of 2,000 pounds, this in a time when a 1906 Cadillac Model K 2-passenger Runabout weighed in at a paltry 1,100 pounds.

The success of the first bus led to the order of another in 1903, and with that the Mack brothers solidified their position as a builder of buses. Custom buses were the order of the day in the early years, but as time wore on it was evident that standardization would be needed in order to increase production. This resulted in two distinct lines, the Senior and the early model Junior. The Mack Senior buses could be distinguished not only by their size, but also by the fact that the Senior line used a right-hand-drive and the Junior line used a left-hand-drive steering system. Power for the first Mack was a four-cylinder of their own design that cranked out a respectable 36 horsepower.

Success came rather easily to the Mack brothers, as they stood in command of their own market. A move from New York to Allentown, Pennsylvania, in 1905 saw the expansion of the company's manufacturing facilities, and output had increased to 51 units for the year. At this point, the name Mack Truck Incorporated was still some years away, and the company was simply called the Mack Brothers Motor Car Company. By maintaining the highest quality standards and manufacturing their own proprietary engines, the Mack brothers were clearly on their way to making a name for themselves in the heavy truck business.

The move to Allentown allowed for a more expanded product line, and Mack soon began to build the trucks for which it would become famous. A 1.5-ton and 2-ton delivery-style truck was built on the bus chassis, while a 5-ton model was available for heavy-duty work. Mack used a new 50-horsepower four-cylinder for the new lineup and, again, quality was the order of the day. Mack's reputation as a builder of durable workhorses was quickly gaining popularity in the early years of the motorcar. A high point was reached in 1911 when output reached 600 trucks and buses. A merger that same year with the Sauer Motor Company saw production

pelled vehicles at the turn of the century. Their first offering would not even be a truck, but a bus for urban transit. This resulted after Augustus Mack took his first ride in a Winton Touring car and came away favorably impressed. The idea of building a car to compete with the Winton and many others in the fledgling automotive industry didn't appeal to the

Mack brothers, as the field of car manufacturers was already crowded. Instead, they decided to appeal to a segment of the market that was largely untapped at that time. The nation was growing, and along with that growth came the need for urban transportation. This resulted in Mack's first offering, called a sight-seeing bus. Although the first Mack resembled nothing

Mack's light-duty pickups were actually overbuilt, with their 7-inch-deep frames and 3⅛-inch-thick side channels.

continue under a financial holding company called The International Motor Company, known simply as IMC. This was followed by the addition of a third manufacturer called the Hewitt Motor Company. This allowed IMC to offer a truck for any commercial need.

Perhaps the greatest benefit brought to

the combination of these three manufacturers was the talents of Edward R. Hewitt and Alfred F. Masury. These two talented engineers would go on to design some of Mack's most popular trucks. Hewitt's design of the Mack Model AB would be so successful that it would be built from 1914 to 1936. Masury would go on to design the

Model AC "Bulldog" Mack that would achieve fame in all facets of the trucking industry. Masury would also be responsible for the design of the famous Mack Bulldog hood ornament that would grace all Mack trucks from 1932 on.

The Mack brothers themselves fell into obscurity after the holding company took over. Over the years, time and market fluctuations took their toll. Eventually, the Sauer and Hewitt line disappeared from the International Motor Company's ranks. With Mack left all alone to carry the IMC banner, it made little sense to have a single company run by a parent company of a different name. On March 22, 1922, IMC's directors voted to change the company name to Mack Trucks Incorporated, and the road was now paved for Mack's domination of the heavy trucking industry.

As Mack approached the mid-thirties, it was no secret that several public works contracts were keeping the company alive through the Depression years. As with most car companies of the era, these were hard times, and many found an alliance with a competitor to be a better fate than death. Sensing a market for a light-duty truck, Mack contracted with REO in October of 1934 to market a pickup truck

Featured on all Mack trucks from 1932 on, the bulldog is a symbol of toughness.

Similar in design to its bigger, 2-ton brother, the little Mack was simply a better-detailed version, albeit in smaller scale.

built by REO. The new Mack Jr. would be identical to REO's light- and medium-duty offerings, save for a few badges and a double trim spear rounding the front radiator. Mack didn't try too hard to hide the Jr.'s lineage, as REO had built a solid reputation with its REO Speedwagon series of 1-ton and 1-1/2-ton trucks.

Mack's new Jr. Model appeared in 1936 and received a restyling just one year later. The first Mack Juniors designated by the letter M were offered in a 1/2-ton model known as the 1M, a 1-1/2 ton model known as a 10M, a 2-ton model known as the 20M, and finally a 3-ton known as the 30M. While the REO and Mack Jr. trucks looked practically identical to one another, that famous Mack bulldog still graced the hood of the Mack Jr.

Marketing of the Mack Jr. allowed the company to penetrate all levels of the public's need for a truck. The Mack Jr. benefited greatly from the company's reputation as a builder of reliable trucks at a time when Mack was still feeling the effects of the Great Depression. The alliance with REO proved to be a success, as Mack would post sales of over 4,000 units for 1936, a figure not seen since 1930.

Realizing the full potential of the light-truck market, Mack began development of its own pickup truck, which would come to be known as the ED series. While the Jr. was truly a light-duty pickup, it could be argued successfully that the Mack ED series was nothing more than a commercial-grade Mack in a diaper. In keeping with Mack's tradition of building heavy-duty trucks, nothing about the ED series was actually light-duty. The ED's frame was constructed of 7-inch-deep, 3-1/6-inch-thick side channels and four cross-members, three of which were boxed and ensured that the ED would not buckle under load. There were distinct styling differences between the Jr. and the ED

Front windshields opened independently to allow fresh air to flow into the cabin.

Mack never used a period after "Jr".

Hood details included four side vents.

series, with the latter benefiting from Mack's vast knowledge of heavy-duty trucks. The ED series was actually an exercise in overkill in terms of a light-duty pickup. The ED series also benefited from a state-of-the-art one-piece windshield, and its quality construction ensured that it would last for many years. With the introduction of the ED series, it became appar-

ent that the writing was on the wall for the Mack Jr. The Jr. was discontinued, and Mack's claim to fame in the light-duty truck market would be solely based on the ED series.

Bill Hurlburt acquired his Mack Jr. in 1995. It had been sitting in a barn for many years, and he made inquires to the owner from time to time. Eventually he got a

phone call back and a deal was struck. The baby Mack was now on its way back to glory. As far as Bill knows, he is only the second owner of this truly unique pickup. This cute little pickup was completely disassembled and treated to a body-off restoration. Some parts were difficult to locate, but in praise of REO's fine engineering, the Mack Jr. was mechanically sound. The most difficult piece to locate was the famous Mack bulldog ornament. While the little doggie himself wasn't too hard to find, the mounting structure that it is perched on is unique to the Mack Jr. Hurlburt eventually gave up and had replacements beautifully crafted by a machinist. The results are outstanding, and everything now looks as it did back in 1937.

Opening the door to the finely restored cab, you quickly notice that you're not in for a luxurious ride. Its utilitarian nature is purely evident from the lack of turn signals and other amenities that are now standard on present-day pickups. Finish your coffee before you leave the house, for you won't find a cup holder in this truck. One imagines that the farmer who originally owned the Jr. would have rested it on the seat or placed it between his legs while shifting. As with most vehicles around the farm, necessity is the mother of invention. Don't bother looking for the heater controls either; it doesn't have one. In 1937, for only $575, the owner of a Mack Jr. got a tough little pickup truck that could do more than earn its keep.

Upon climbing into the cab of the Mack Jr. it is apparent that one is entering a pickup from the 1930s. Its basic interior speaks of a time when the pickup truck was a machine of simplicity. Forget about leather interiors and console-mounted entertainment centers, the Mack Jr. is a true pickup that was built long before the popularity of the SUV. The first thing you notice is that the seat is bolted into position. Despite the lack of an adjustment, it seems to be comfortable for anyone between five- and six-feet tall. Owner Bill Hurlburt's 6-foot 3-inch frame fits comfortably into the cab with just a few inches of head room to spare. Posture in the Mack Jr.'s firm seat is just right. Unlike a modern automobile, the Mack allows the rider's legs to bend and lets the feet rest flat on the floor. It's more like sitting on the living room sofa than riding in a truck. Visibility through the split front windshield is excellent, and the reassuring posture of the bulldog up front gives the driver a sense of confidence and reliability.

My own thoughts upon entering the Mack's cab take me back to high school,

TRUCKING IN THE THIRTIES

Trucking in 1937 was more like an adventure than an actual job. The comforts of the modern-day sleeper cab were uncommon, and long hours at the wheel of a primitive truck were hard on the human body. There were approximately 2,500 diesel trucks on the road in 1937, and trains were still hauling much of the nation's cargo.

The Automotive Safety Foundation was organized in 1937 to promote vehicle safety, and that same year, the Interstate Commerce Commission created several new regulations designed to toughen the standards for driver qualifications and safety equipment. The regulatory requirements covered brakes, tire chains, fire extinguishers, flares, fuel tanks, glass, headlamps, mirrors, and windshield wipers. The safety features of a modern over-the-road-truck can trace their lineage to these very standards.

The West Coast consumed more diesel fuel that the East Coast in 1937, thanks to the wide-open roads and less restrictive weight limits. The current design trend was for all-metal bodies with strength and weight tak-

ing center stage in truck manufacturing. International Harvester offered no less than 26 different models on its D lineup, and the famous Walter Snow Fighter offered "four-point positive drive" in its four-wheel-drive units. The Walter is still thought of today by many veteran truckers as the ultimate snow-plow truck. GMC offered a full line of cab-over-engine models that were both reliable and attractive. Many car companies were looking for a piece of the action, with Hudson announcing the availability of a 3/4-ton "Big Boy" commercial truck and Studebaker adding a Hercules diesel engine to its truck line.

The American truck industry was growing fast in 1937, as the nation's goods were transported all over the country. In just a few years, the American truck would go to war, and many trucks would see service in Europe and other theaters in World War II. Surplus war trucks would turn up all over the world in the following decades, and a military jeep or truck never fails to turn heads at a local car show.

when I owned a 1967 International 1100B pickup. The same utilitarian nature is present in both trucks. I often say to many generation X'ers that, "I've been driving pickups since before they were cool to drive." But the Mack has something that my old International didn't have: charm. The cute lines of the Mack Jr. are a show-stopper everywhere it goes.

Familiarization with the gauges and gearshift controls is easy, given the simple nature of the dash layout. The gauges are nicely designed and very easy to read. The smart-looking instrument pod on the left holds an oil-pressure gauge in the 12 o'clock position. Fuel is at 3 o'clock, amps are at 6 o'clock, and temperature rounds out the circle at 9. The speedometer is conveniently located just to the right, and it takes only a quick glance to read it. The Jr. is equipped with only one door-mounted rear-view mirror, and it is actually harder to look in the rear-view than it is to check the gauges. There is nothing about the Mack's interior that suggests comfort, but then we're here to work, not to be pampered with the comforts of leather interiors and automatic transmissions.

Starting the Mack Jr. is as simple as turning the key and depressing the starter switch located in the center of the floorboard. Its Continental straight-six starts immediately and doesn't exactly roar to life, but begins its leisurely purr as if to say, "I'm ready, let's go." The engine is remarkably smooth and quiet, with no vibration evident in the body or steering wheel. The tell-tale indicator of any good truck is to look in the rear-view mirror with the engine at idle. If it vibrates, you need a tune-up or a better truck. The Jr.'s rear-view mirror is rock steady as the engine awaits it command. The Jr. has a steadiness in its mechanical components that would rival any modern automobile.

Clutch travel is minimal; only about one-inch off the floor and the Jr. responds with ease. The shifting pattern is as easy as it gets. First gear is toward the driver and down, reverse is straight up, second is over and up away from the driver and third is straight down. As I ease the clutch out, there isn't a hint of hesitation to be found. The Jr. is surging ahead as its 72 horsepower engine brings the pickup to life. Shifting into second is just as easy and, to this driver's credit, the gear change is without any grinding or chatter. Second feels like a good pulling gear, and the pickup brings itself up to speed with ease. Topping off in third gear the Jr. is in its element, cruising along without even working hard. Once up to speed, noise increases somewhat, but this is a pickup

Basic metal step finished in black enamel.

Carburetor is a one-barrel plain tube type.

that makes no promises except to get you there and back.

This little Mack beauty traverses the back roads of Northwest Connecticut with ease. Hills are no problem, and cornering is very responsive. The truck is genuinely tight with very few squeaks and rattles, and these only occur at high speed. We inquire later as to what was replaced on the Jr. during its restoration to make it ride so nice, and Bill tells us that he "replaced almost nothing." He merely disassembled and cleaned all of the suspension compo-

nents, then put everything back together just as it was. The Mack's ride is no doubt a tribute to REO's experience in building passenger cars since 1905. Indeed, the ride is very similar to that of a passenger car of the same era.

Steering is very good, and the truck is surprisingly responsive. Again, Bill says that he did "nothing to the steering box during restoration," but he also pulled it out of its deep slumber, with only 19,000 miles showing on its odometer. As a New England squirrel darts out in front of us,

Continental L-head straight-six develops 144-lbs.ft. of torque below 2,000 rpm.

Two large, light gray-faced gauges with their chrome bezels contrast nicely with red dash.

Three-hinge hood opens in typical fashion.

Simple yet stylish chromed exterior door handles feature integral lock.

the Jr.'s steering is put to the test, and it passes with flying colors. The Mack swerves confidently, and the squirrel lives to see another New England day. One almost begins to believe that we could do the cone treatment at any high-speed driving course, but the Jr. is content to putter along at its own pace.

If the Mack Jr. lacks in anything, it is stopping ability. As with any car of its era, it lets you know rather quickly that it's not disc brake-equipped. It is certainly good enough to halt the pickup when stopping is foreseen, but one wonders what it would do in a panic, especially with a load of dirt or rocks on board. The brake pedal is not hard to find, and ample room is provided on the Jr.'s floor for foot space when not using it. It is not hard to get used to the brakes, given enough time, but there's one motion that you'll never get used to. Every time we make a turn, my hand reaches for a signal indicator that is not, and will never be there. The Jr. was built without turn signals, and in the interest of authenticity, Bill decided to leave it as is.

We pull back into Bill's yard, and our drive is over all too quickly. I can't help but compare the Mack Jr.'s size to Bill's fleet of logging trucks. The Jr. is dwarfed by Bill's 1987 Mack DM Tri-axle dump truck and a 1989 Mack RD tandem, complete with a log-loader, which he uses in the nearby Berkshire Mountains. Big heavy-duty Macks are what Bill usually drives, so maneuvering the little Jr. is like a walk in the park for him. Turning off the engine, you have to just sit for a little while and marvel at the wonderfully simplistic nature of the Jr. It's a pure joy to drive, and its effortless mechanical systems only add to its charisma. What it lacks in creature comforts is more than made up for in its devotion to simplicity. It literally defines an era when an engine was not saddled with air-conditioning units and anti-pollution gizmos. No power accessories or carpet here, just good solid transportation. It's a charming pickup that could make a home for itself in anyone's garage. ☞

THE COMPETITION

Make Model	Mack Jr. Model 2M	Dodge MC 1/2-ton	Chevy GC 1/2-ton	Ford Model 73	Studebaker Coupe Express J5
Price	$575	$540	$515	$516	$647
Engine	209-cu.in. Inline-6	281-cu.in. Inline-6	206.8-cu.in. Inline-6	136-cu.in. V-8	217.8-cu.in. Inline-6
Horsepower	72	75	79	60	86
Transmission	3-speed	3-speed	3-speed	3-speed	3-speed
Wheelbase	114 inches	116 inches	112-1/2 inches	112 inches	116 inches
Weight	2,975 lbs.	2,700 lbs.	2,805 lbs.	2,397 lbs.	3,168 lbs.

illustrations by Russell von Sauers, The Graphic Automobile Studio
© copyright 2002, Special Interest Autos

specifications

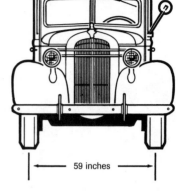

114 inches

59 inches

1937 Mack Jr Model 2M

Base price	$575
Std. equipment	Cab w/safety glass, rear fenders, front bumper, tail-lamps, rear-view mirror, shock absorbers
Options on dR truck	None

ENGINE

Type	Continental L-head straight-six
Bore x stroke	3.1875 inches x 4.375 inches
Displacement	209 cubic inches
Horsepower @ rpm	72 @ 3,000
Torque @ rpm	144 lbs.ft. @ 800–2,000
Compression ratio	5.4:1
Cylinder block	Chrome Nickel
Cylinders	Cast en bloc with detachable one-piece head
Connecting rods	Manganese steel
Valves	L-head, 30-degree seat
Main bearings	4
Total bearing area	41.97 sq. in.
Fuel feed	Mechanical pump
Lubrication system	Full force-feed through rifle drilled oil passages
Exhaust system	Single

TRANSMISSION

Type	Warner Gear 84C 3-speed manual, helical countershaft drive

Gear ratios:	1st	2.57:1
	2nd	1.55:1
	High	1.00:1
	Reverse	3.48:1

CLUTCH

Type	Heavy dry single-plate, 9.875-inch diameter
Frictional area	94.25 square inches

DIFFERENTIAL

Type	Hotchkiss drive
Ratio	4.5:1

BRAKES

Type	Drum, internal expanding
Front and rear	11 x 1.75-inch drum diameter
Swept area	85 square inches
Hand brake	External on transmission, 6x2 inches
Swept area	37.125 sq. in.
Total swept area	207.125 sq. in.

STEERING

Type	Cam-and-lever
Turning diameter	20.6 feet

CHASSIS & BODY

Body	Steel
Chassis	Steel ladder frame

Body style	Pickup with bed
Layout	Front engine, rear drive

SUSPENSION

Front	Tube shocks, leaf springs, 8 leaves, 36 x 1.75 inches
Rear	Tube shocks, leaf springs, 9 leaves, 54 x 1.75 inches
Tires	6.00 x 16-in. front/rear
Wheels	Pressed steel disc

WEIGHTS AND MEASURES

Wheelbase	114 inches
Overall length	174 inches
Overall width	49.125 inches
Overall height	77 inches
Front track	59 inches
Rear track	61 inches
Gross vehicle weight rating	4,500 pounds

CAPACITIES

Cooling system	14 quarts
Fuel tank	16 gallons

Mack engine plate located on block shows its New York origin.

Express Delivery

Hauling goods in style, in a
1947 Studebaker M-5 Coupe Express pickup

by Arch Brown
Photography by Bud Juneau

Originally published in Special Interest Autos #173, Sept.-Oct. 1999

Studebaker had a long, if somewhat checkered history in the commercial vehicle market. Nearly a century and a half ago, the company had built its reputation largely on the strength of its sturdy freight and farm wagons. Then in the early years of the Twentieth Century, a line of electric delivery vehicles was featured, ranging in capacity from 500 pounds to three tons. The problem here, as with all electric vehicles both then and now, was their limited range. Typically, about 30 miles appears to have been the limit before the batteries required recharging.

A handful of gasoline-powered trucks using the Garford chassis were built, commencing in about 1907, but the Garford was an expensive machine, and it wasn't until the company's association with EMF (Everett-Metzger-Flanders) in 1908 that Studebaker marketed commercial vehicles in significant numbers. The EMF and its companion marque, the Flanders, were plagued at first by snapped driveshafts, reportedly resulting from the two-speed, rear axle-mounted transmission that was then employed. This, incidentally led to what is believed to have been the industry's first factory recall, in 1910, when the two-speed transmissions were replaced with three-speed gearboxes.

During 1911 the Studebaker Brothers Manufacturing Company merged with EMF to form the Studebaker Corporation, and over the next three seasons a half-ton, 20-horsepower Flanders delivery was marketed. Then in 1914 a much stronger, 3/4-ton, 30 horsepower delivery was offered, this time bearing the Studebaker name.

Evidently this enterprise failed to be as profitable as company officials may have wished, for when the 1918 models appeared, the commercial units had been dropped from the line. Larger models appeared seven years later, but it wasn't until 1927 that Studebaker light-duty delivery vehicles reappeared, accompanied this time by a few Erskine units. This range remained in production through 1931, after which it was replaced by smartly styled and highly competent delivery vehicles from Studebaker's Rockne subsidiary.

But, as Studebaker authority Fred Fox has noted, "It wasn't until the introduction of the Coupe Express pickup in 1937 that the company gained recognition for being a producer of light-duty trucks." The secret was in the styling, the work of the famed Raymond Loewy.

Built on the 116-inch wheelbase of the Dictator Series passenger cars, but equipped with two-stage springs in order to handle the extra loads with

"The 1937 Coupe Express proved to be the most popular truck Studebaker had ever built, with production reaching 3,125 units."

which pickup trucks are often burdened, the Coupe Express was easily the handsomest light truck on the market. Having been based on passenger car styling, it was fitted with vent windows in the doors, a feature not usually offered in pickups of that era. The sturdy double-walled, six-foot pickup box was made of 16-gauge steel, and a steel bed-floor was used. The spare tire was mounted in a right-front fender well, where it was much more accessible than the customary under-the-bed placement. Other features, unusual in a vehicle of this type, included dual inside sun visors, dome light, rear-view mirror, adjustable seat, and even the familiar, and very useful, Studebaker "hill-holder." Overdrive, radio, heater, electric clock, fog lamps and spotlight were items available at extra cost.

The Dictator engine was ideally suited for use in a pickup truck. With a displacement of 217.8 cubic inches, it was rated at 86 horsepower, and it developed 160 foot-pounds of torque at 1,200 rpm. The hypoid semi-floating rear axle carried a standard ratio of 4.55:1, although the optional 4.82:1 cogs were often fitted in combination with the overdrive.

The 1937 Coupe Express proved to be the most popular truck Studebaker had ever built, up to that time, with production reaching 3,125 units. But, of course, that figure couldn't come close to matching the numbers being turned out by Chevrolet, Ford and even Dodge. The reason is not far to seek, for the Studebaker's factory price was $647. And however reasonable that figure may seem today, in its own time it was a bit pricey compared, say, to the $515 Chevrolet or the $525 Ford.

By 1938 the Dictator name had begun to have very unpleasant connotations, and the time-honored Commander title was called out of retirement to replace it. Once again there was a Studebaker Coupe Express, employing passenger car sheet metal as well as the running gear of the re-titled Commander series. But 1938 was a recession year, and sales dropped off to an even 1,000 units.

Studebaker gave it one more try for 1939, producing what some regard as the best looking edition of the Coupe Express. But the price, this time, was $850, and although times were better than they had been in 1938, for most pickup buyers that kind of money was not easy to justify at a time when the half-ton Chevrolet pickup could be purchased for $572 or a Ford for $570. Only 1,200 of the handsome Studebaker haulers were produced that year.

Evidently Studebaker's management thought it was time to stop and catch their collective breath, for there was no Coupe Express—no pickup truck under any title—for 1940. But capitalizing on the success of the economical little Champion passenger cars that had been such a hit from the time of their introduction in mid-1939, for 1941 they introduced the Champion-based M5 pickup,

again using the Coupe Express title.

This time, although the truck was attractive enough, it made no pretense of being based on passenger-car styling; and instead of the Commander engine, it was powered by the 169.6-cubic-inch, 80-horsepower flathead of the little Champion. An I-beam front axle was substituted for the Champion's "Planar" independent front suspension, and fittings were generally much plainer than those of the earlier Coupe Express models. A single sun visor was supplied, for example, and one windshield wiper in place of the earlier duals. But for buyers with an extra $24.47 to spend, there was a dress-up package that included a stainless steel grille bar overlay, hood ornament, bright metal side moldings, and fenders painted in the body color, rather than in black.

Production of the Coupe-Express was suspended "for the duration" on January 31, 1942; and although truck production was resumed on a limited basis during the spring of 1945, the government permitted Studebaker to build only the M15 one-ton units. It happened that the 80-horsepower Champion engine had remained in production throughout the war, for it had been used to power the amphibious M-29 Weasels that had proved so useful in the swamps of the South Pacific. So all of Studebaker's wartime civilian trucks—and the postwar models as well—employed the small "six," rather than the larger unit of the Commander models.

Only after the war ended did the M-5 Coupe-Express return to the line. And when it did, the postwar Studebaker trucks were virtually identical to their

Clamshell-styled hood helped increase engine accessibility considerably.

With the overdrive engaged, M-5 cruises comfortably at a steady 60 mph; although it leans a little, wide track helps maintain control.

Chrome hubcap accentuates 16-inch size.

Spare tire is housed below the bed floor, while tailgate makes great billboard.

prewar counterparts. The M-5 was evidently an economical unit to produce, which suggests that it must have been profitable for the company. The dashboard, for example, was borrowed from the prewar Champion passenger cars; no additional tooling costs there. Fenders were interchangeable, front-to-rear on the same side, while running boards interchanged from left side to right. Hubcaps were borrowed from the Studebaker Commander.

Options included, among other items, overdrive, hill-holder (no longer on the standard equipment list), radio, heater, electric clock, interior rear view mirror, dual horns, turn signals, windshield washers, chrome rear bumper, bumper guards, heavy-duty bumper, wheel trim rings, glove compartment light, vacuum booster for the windshield wiper, right inside visor and a right-side taillamp.

The M-5 was 14 inches shorter, overall, than the 1939 Coupe Express, and 590 pounds lighter. Yet it had a full-sized six and a half-foot bed; and best of all, it sold, during 1947 for $644, just $44 more than the Chevrolet and $39 more than the Ford. And it sold well. Studebaker produced 67,811 light and medium-duty trucks during 1947, of which approximately 23,377 were half-ton M-5 Coupe Express units. These numbers, representing a single year's work, were greater than the total of all motorized commercial vehicles produced by Studebaker during the years before World War II. Exact figures for the succeeding years are not available, but it appears that 1947 may have been Studebaker's high-water mark as far as the commercial vehicle market was concerned.

Of course, Studebaker was riding the crest of the postwar "seller's market" at

WHERE TO FIND ONE

If you are thinking of adding an M-5 Coupe Express to your vehicle collection, be prepared for a long, hard search. These distinctive looking trucks are hard to find, especially in solid condition with all their original trim pieces in good shape. Your best bet is to join the Studebaker Drivers Club, since their monthly magazine is loaded with classifieds of cars and trucks for sale. Over the course of the last six months, in *Hemmings Motor News,* we discovered one M-5 for sale. The ad read: 1947 M-5 1/2-ton Pickup, runs, $2,150. And if all else fails, just place a "Wanted" ad in the "S" Wanted section of *Hemmings Motor News*; you're almost guaranteed to find the M-5 of your dreams.

The M-5 is a well-proportioned 1/2-ton pickup truck, with a clean, compact style.

Chromed license plate frame with integrated light housing artfully designed.

Headlight bezel incorporates turn signal.

CLUB CORNER

Antique Studebaker Club
P.O. Box 28845
Dallas, TX 75228
972-709-6185
Dues: $23./year
Publishes the Studebaker Review *every month, hosts a yearly national meet plus several zone meets.*

Studebaker Drivers Club
P.O. Box 28788
Dallas, TX 75228
800-527-3452
Dues: $27.50/year
The world's largest Studebaker club with 13,000-plus members, publishes the Turning Wheels *magazine every month.*

that time. Demand was at an unprecedented level. Yet company officials knew that a less favorable market would inevitably come; so during the spring of 1948 a freshly styled truck line, designed by the talented Bob Bourke—the man who would ultimately be responsible for the stunning Starlight Coupes—was introduced. Officially, these trucks were known as the "2R" series, but the company, recalling the pioneer days when John Studebaker had spent five years establishing the family fortune in Placerville, better known as "Old Hangtown," in the heart of the California Gold Rush country, advertised the new trucks as "The 49'ers."

The Bourke-designed trucks were beyond question the best-looking trucks then on the market. But still, only the Champion engine was offered, though the larger Commander unit had been back in production for passenger-car use since the spring of 1946. This was an incomprehensible mistake, for when it came to performance—as we have seen—the Champion-powered Studebaker trucks simply could not compete. That problem was finally remedied during April 1950, when the larger, 102-horsepower engine joined the option list. But it's our guess that during that time, Studebaker had lost some ground that it never really managed to regain.

During 1948, when I was teaching at a rural California high school, I had occasion to drive a one-ton Studebaker M-15 heavy-duty stake truck. The experience came about because I was moving my family from a rather raunchy rental to a more desirable home in another part of the community. My monthly salary at the time was $266.67. Pretty good pay for a beginning teacher in those days, but it didn't leave much for such extras as moving expenses. Happily for us, the town grocer, Walt Billigmeier, offered me the use of his

specifications

1947 Studebaker M-5 Coupe Express

← 113 inches →

← 59.9 inches →

Original price	$1,082 f.o.b. factory, with standard equipment
Options on dR car	Overdrive, hill-holder, radio, heater, wheel trim rings, white sidewall tires, twin spotlights outside sun visor, fog lamps, chromed rear bumper, chromed grille, front bumper guards, outside mirror, turn signals, locking gas cap, dashboard clock, dual windshield wipers, exhaust extension, steering wheel spinner knob

ENGINE

Type	L-head 6-cylinder, cast in block
Bore x stroke	3 inches x 4 inches
Displacement	169.6 cubic inches
Compression ratio	6.5:1
Horsepower @ rpm	80 @ 4,000
Torque @ rpm	134 @ 2,000
Taxable horsepower	21.6
Valve lifters	Hydraulic
Main bearings	4
Valve lifters	Mechanical
Lubrication system	Pressure
Fuel system	Single downdraft carburetor, camshaft pump
Cooling system	Centrifugal pump
Exhaust system	Single
Electrical system	6-volt battery/coil

TRANSMISSION

Type	3-speed selective with optional overdrive
Ratios: 1st	1st: 2.66:1; 2nd: 1.56:1; 3rd: 1.00:1; Reverse: 3.55:1
Overdrive	0.72:1

CLUTCH

Type	Single dry disc
Outside diameter	9.5 inches
Actuation	Mechanical, foot pedal

REAR AXLE

Type	Hypoid
Ratio	4.82:1
Drive axles	Semi-floating

STEERING

Type	Ross cam-and-lever
Ratio	Variable
Turns lock-to-lock	4
Turning radius	20' 3" left; 20' 0" right

BRAKES

Type	4-wheel internal hydraulic, drum type
Drum diameter	11 inches
Effective area	177.5 square inches

CHASSIS & BODY

Construction	Body-on-frame
Frame	Channel iron with 6 cross members
Body construction	All steel
Body type	1/2-ton pickup

SUSPENSION

Front	I-beam axle, semi-elliptic springs
Rear	Rigid axle, semi-elliptic springs
Shock absorbers	Delco-Lovejoy single-acting hydraulic
Tires	6.50 x 16 inch 6-ply
Wheels	Steel disc

WEIGHTS AND MEASURES

Wheelbase	113 inches
Overall length	181.25 inches
Overall width	75.3 inches
Overall height	77 inches
Front track	59.9 inches
Rear track	59.6 inches
Min. road clearance	7.75 inches
Curb weight	2,635 pounds

CARGO BED DIMENSIONS

Length	78.2 inches
Width	48.5 inches
Height	13.4 inches

CAPACITIES

Crankcase	5 quarts
Cooling system	10.5 quarts
Fuel tank	18 gallons
Transmission	1 lb. plus 2.2 lb. overdrive
Rear axle	2 lb.

CALCULATED DATA

Stroke/bore ratio	1.33:1
Weight per hp	32.9 pounds
Weight per c.i.d.	15.5 pounds
Lb. per sq. in. (brakes)	14.8

Studebaker truck in order to haul our belongings from one house to the other. For that favor I have always been profoundly grateful to Walt.

But my impression of that truck, which as I recall had a four-speed transmission, was that it could scarcely get out of its own way. No surprise here, for a one-ton stake-back is no lightweight, and Walt's truck, like all Studebaker light- and medium-duty trucks of that era, was powered by the 169.6-cubic-inch Champion engine. Talk about sending a boy to do a man's work! But I had no complaints. One didn't dare drive the Studebaker any faster than

about 40 miles an hour, but we weren't traveling any great distance, so the truck got the job done for us. And saved us moving costs that had looked like a king's ransom to a young couple with a small child.

So when the opportunity recently presented itself, I was delighted to take the

wheel of Carl Poteet's half-ton Studebaker Coupe Express. On the face of it, this unit had to be a much better performer than Walt Billigmeier's big one-tonner. And in lieu of the big truck's four-speed transmission, the Coupe Express is equipped with a three-speed gearbox—plus overdrive, which was bound to be something of an advantage, at least on the open road. As one might expect, both Billigmeier's four-speed and Poteet's overdrive were optional at extra cost.

Poteet's Coupe Express has been completely rebuilt mechanically, so its performance approximates about as closely as possible, that of a new vehicle. A flick of the ignition switch is followed by depressing the clutch in order to activate the starter. This practice, originated by Nash in 1934 and adopted by Studebaker a few years later, strikes me as one of the better ideas, for two reasons. First, it's impossible to start the vehicle in gear, an important safety factor; and second, in the event of a stall the engine can be re-started without the driver having to take his hands off the wheel.

The clutch on this particular truck is adjusted in such a way that it engages the moment the driver lets up even fractionally on the pedal. So it has to be depressed all the way to the floor—that's ALL the way—before the shift can be made to low gear. We found that to be a trifle disconcerting, but of course the problem has to do with the adjustment in this particular unit, and is not a Studebaker characteristic.

Once the shift to low gear is accomplished, the clutch action is smooth, and pedal pressure is not excessive. I remember reading somewhere that these pickups featured column-mounted shift levers, but this one has a floor shift. It's an easy gearbox to use, requiring little effort as it is changed from gear to gear. It is also a quiet transmission, and the synchronizers on second and third speeds are quite effective.

Acceleration is obviously better than the big M-15 units, but this truck is no hotshot performer. Once up to speed, however, it cruises smoothly and without complaint at 60 miles an hour with the overdrive engaged. But when it comes to climbing hills it's clearly short on torque. (A glance at the accompanying comparison table tells the story: The

Chromed grille was optional.

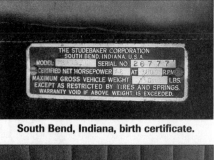
South Bend, Indiana, birth certificate.

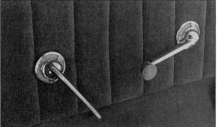
Simple but elegant interior handles.

Studebaker's torque measures 134 foot pounds, compared to anywhere from 172 to 180 for competing makes.)

Given that an I-beam axle is used in lieu of independent front suspension, the ride is surprisingly smooth. Seats are comfortable and supportive. The little Studebaker leans some in the turns, and the driver is acutely aware that this truck is taller than it is wide; yet it's easy enough to maintain control, perhaps because of its relatively wide track, which measures 59.9 inches front, 59.6 inches rear.

Steering is moderately heavy, and it is at this point that I realized why owner Carl Poteet equipped this pickup with a "spinner" device on the steering wheel. The "spinner" was a popular aftermarket option during the 1930s and '40s. As kids we called them "wrist crackers,"

or even "Ritz crackers," and found them useful when driving with one hand while the right arm was wrapped around a young lady. Problem was, if you let go of the wheel and permitted it to center itself, as the wheel spun around the knob sometimes collided painfully with the driver's wrist.

In the case of Carl Poteet's Studebaker, I found to my discomfort that the spotlight control came so close to the steering wheel that if I rounded a turn with my hands on the wheel rather than using the spinner, I was inviting a set of pinched fingers. I learned that lesson rather quickly, and made good use of the spinner.

The brakes are very good. Studebaker provided larger drums and more lining area for the Coupe Express than for the Champion passenger cars whose engine

1947 STUDEBAKER M-5 VERSUS THE COMPETITION

Make	Studebaker	Chevrolet	Dodge	Ford
Model	M-5 Coupe Express	3100 Pickup	WC Pickup	79C Pickup
Price, 1/2 ton pickup	$1,082	$1,087	$989	$1,143
Wheelbase	113 inches	116 inches	116 inches	114 inches
Weight (lb.)	2,635	3,205	2,975	2,921
Overall length	181 1/4 inches	196 1/2 inches	191 3/8 inches	188 3/4 inches
Bed length	78 1/4 inches	78 inches	78 1/8 inches	78 inches
Engine	6-cyl.	6-cyl.	6-cyl.	V-8*
Displacement (cu. in.)	169.6	216.5	217.8	239.4
Horsepower/rpm	80/4,000	90/3,300	95/3,600	100/3,800
Torque/rpm	134/2,000	174/1,200-2,000	172/1,200	180/2,000
Compression ratio	6.50:1	6.50:1	6.60:1	6.20:1
Valve configuration	L-head	OHV	L-head	L-head
Final drive ratio	4.82:1	4.11:1	4.10:1	3.92:1
Overdrive available?	Optional	No	No	No
Tire size	6.50/16	6.00/16	6.00/16	6.50/16
Stroke/bore ratio	1.33:1	1.07:1	1.35:1	1.18:1
Horsepower per c.i.d.	.472	.416	.436	.418
Weight (lb.) per h.p.	32.9	35.6	31.3	29.2
Weight per c.i.d.	15.5	14.8	13.7	12.2

* Note: The Ford was also available with a 225.8 cu.in. 6-cylinder, L-head engine rated at 95 horsepower and 180 pounds-feet of torque @ 1200 rpm. Compression ratio was 6.70:1. Price was $15 less than the V-8.

The dashboard was borrowed from the prewar Champion passenger cars.

Deco-inspired Quad Duty radio optional.

Amperes, gas, speedo, oil & temp gauges.

the little truck borrowed. Stops are straight and smooth, and the relatively generous lining area suggests that brake-fade should not be a problem.

Overall, the Coupe Express appears to be a sturdy unit, and it would certainly be economical to operate as well as easy to drive. But I'm still persuaded that it would be a much more desirable vehicle if it were powered by a larger engine. Evidently Studebaker eventually reached that conclusion too, for commencing on April 11, 1950, a Commander-powered pickup joined the line. And it cost only $50.00 more than the Champion-engined version.

The Coupe Express featured here was purchased in 1961 by Oleanan Poteet, father of its present owner, Carl Poteet, of Yuba City, California. The elder Poteet used it for some fifteen years, hauling almonds to market from his ranch. And then it sat, literally, in a chicken house until 1986, when Carl came to its rescue. The speedometer registered 86,000 miles at that time, but when one considers that the pickup was then more than forty years old, there is no way of telling what the actual mileage may have been.

Carl gave the pickup a complete ground-up restoration, both cosmetic and mechanical. It had been delivered with virtually no optional equipment, but Carl dressed it up with nearly every accessory in Studebaker's book, along with a few aftermarket items such as the outside sun visor and the side-

boards shown here. One additional feature was added: The original interior could only be described as "Spartan." During the restoration, simply as a matter of personal preference, Carl had it substantially upgraded.

The restoration was completed by 1989, and Carl promptly took it to a Studebaker Drivers Club meet in Las Vegas, where it won top honors in its class. Since that time, the little Studebaker has been used strictly for show, and not for everyday transportation, not to mention hauling almonds. Today, ten years following its restoration, the truck remains in "show" condition; and over the years it has picked up several additional awards. A ritual that is likely to continue, not only because of its outstanding quality of restoration, but also because of the M-5's fine design and appealing style, which seems to attract the public's approval wherever it goes. ◯

Bibliography

Automobile Editors of Consumer Guide, Collectible and Classic Trucks; Automotive Industries, *various issues;* Cannon, *William A. and Fred K. Fox,* Studebaker, the Complete Story; Gunnell, *John A. (ed.),* Standard Catalog of American Light Duty Trucks; *Hall, Asa E. and Richard M. Langworth,* The Studebaker Century; *Langworth, Richard M.,* Illustrated Studebaker Buyer's Guide; *Studebaker factory literature;* "Studebaker M-5 Coupe Express." Collectible Automobile, February 1991.

1937 TERRAPLANE
UTILITY COUPE PICKUP

by John Lee
photos by the author

THE traveling salesman, besides being the subject of innumerable jokes, was also the object of the car dealer's affection in the 1930s. These knights of the road accounted for a significant number of new car sales.

Long before 800 numbers and FAX machines, hundreds of Willy Lomans packed the trunks of their cars full of samples and catalogs on Monday morning and headed out for the "territory." Up and down the highways they drove, calling on customers in every town and spending their nights in cheap hotels. They'd plan their trip to be back home Saturday night, in time for the wives to launder their clothes so they'd be ready to do it all over again Monday morning.

The auto industry was well aware of this category of consumer. He put more miles on a car in a year than the average family did in three, which meant he'd be back to buy a new model much more often. As cars progressed to fully enclosed, all-steel bodies and more special-purpose models entered the lineup, some were specifically directed toward the traveling salesman.

The sedan delivery with a cargo area accessed through a swinging rear door had been hauling loads for some years.

Several manufacturers had added a utility sedan, which retained the top-hinged trunk door and the rear side windows (sometimes covered by removable panels), but had removable rear and right front seats to create a cargo deck rivaling that of the sedan delivery.

Most popular was the business coupe, with a two-passenger bench seat in front and a massive trunk in back.

Hudson described how their business coupe, or utility coupe differed from the passenger coupe:

"1. Seat — Back of seat is divided so that back folds forward, permitting easy access to compartment just in rear of seat. 2. Spare tire carrier — Spare tire is carried vertically in recess...built just back of seat. 3. Rear compartment — By carrying spare tire in recess back of seat, the rear compartment is unobstructed and provides large load area. There is no 'sill' or obstruction above floor level." The utility coupe's trunk was five and a half feet deep and four feet wide.

Then, for 1937, Hudson introduced a new wrinkle in its Terraplane line: a fold-out pickup box. The steel box, measuring 49½ inches long, 38 inches wide, and 11½ inches deep, rolled on tracks, similar to a file cabinet drawer. Pushed all the way in, it fit entirely inside the trunk compartment and was concealed by the top-hinged decklid. For either loading or hauling, it could be pulled out to a point just inside the rear bumper or to its full extension eight inches beyond the bumper. The tailgate, like that of an ordinary pickup, dropped down to bed level and was supported by chains for loading, unloading or carrying long loads. Extra tall or bulky loads were accommodated by removing the decklid.

Hudson didn't pioneer this concept. Plymouth offered a removable pickup box for its business coupe from 1935 through 1939. Chevrolet had a similar option from 1937 through 1939 and Pontiac for 1937 and 1938, but no one promoted it as a separate model like Terraplane did. They called it the utility coupe pickup and gave it a half-ton load rating.

THE CAR WITH A DRAWER IN THE BACK

Hudson's commercial vehicle endeavors had been up and down over the years. The pioneer automaker had built utility vehicles for the military during World War I. In the 1920s the Cotton Motor Company of Boston offered the Cotton-Beverly open wood station wagon-style body on the Essex chassis to Hudson-Essex dealers. A dealer could also order a chassis from Hudson and have it shipped to Cantrell to be fitted with a similar Cantrell Suburban body.

In 1929 Hudson expanded into the commercial field with the new Dover line of light commercial vehicles — a panel delivery, screenside express, open express, canopy express, and a sedan delivery, in addition to a bare chassis on which a body of the buyer's choice could be constructed. Dovers used Essex fenders, headlamps, running boards, hood, cowl, and front-opening doors. The commercial line switched to the Essex nameplate for 1930 and struggled along into the early part of the Depression.

By 1933 the Essex name was being phased out in favor of the new Terraplane, an Essex series introduced in 1932 that gained immediate appeal with its low cost and the highest power-to-weight ratio in the industry. By 1934, when all reference to the Essex name

Facing page: With drawer fully extended, coupe has the capacity of a small pickup bed. *Above:* It looks like a regular Terraplane with lid closed. *Below:* Distinctive grille extends past leading edge of hood.

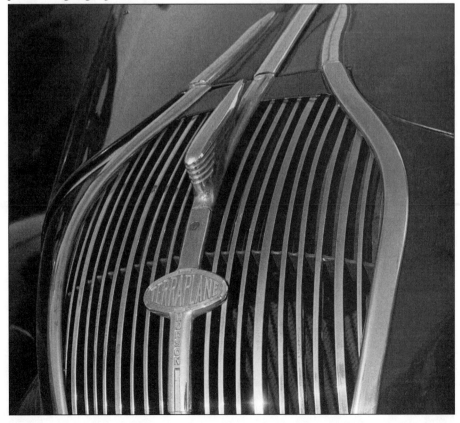

1937 TERRAPLANE

Above: Tidy gauge layout has speedo which shows velocity reading in an unusual anticlockwise direction. *Below:* Who needs a hatchback when you have this kind of utility?

had been dropped, sales of the Terraplane commercial line soared to 1,901 units, a 342 percent increase over the previous model year. Models that year were the utility coach, sedan delivery, cab pickup express with the passenger car front end and half-ton capacity, a wood station wagon body by Cantrell and a chassis with or without cab.

Commercial sales fell off again in 1935, in spite of 3/4-ton capacity delivery and pickup express models being added. Four finished commercial models and two chassis were available when Hudsons and Terraplanes got new, rounded, flowing body lines for the 1936 model year. A new eight-passenger custom station wagon joined the cab pickup express, custom panel delivery, and utility coach.

Hudson made an even greater commitment to commercial vehicles for 1937 and was rewarded with record sales of 8,058 units, a 77.1 percent increase over 1936. The new utility coupe pickup, with half-ton rating, fit into the Series 70 with the custom panel delivery, utility coach, station wagon, and cab pickup. All were built on a new 117-inch wheelbase, a two-inch increase from 1936.

In addition, there was a new Big Boy line consisting of a custom panel delivery, cab pickup, taxi cab and chassis with or without cab. Big Boys were built on a longer, 124-inch wheelbase and rated at 3/4-ton capacity.

With its 212-cubic-inch L-head six cranking out 96 horsepower, Hudson had the most powerful light utility vehicles. A channel section frame and longitudinal leaf spring suspension with an I-beam front axle and solid rear axle made up the simple, sturdy platform.

The phase-out of Terraplane began in 1938, when it was designated as a Hudson series rather than a separate marque. Thus, both Hudson and Terraplane nameplates appeared on those models, which included the utility coupe pickup. Nearly identical models were offered in the new, economy Hudson 112 line. The group was known as Hudson business cars.

The same line-up of commercials continued for 1939 and 1940, without the Terraplane name. By now the coupe with the drawer in the trunk was grouped with the utility coach, station wagon and taxi as the Traveler series.

New front-end styling for 1940 was slightly altered again for 1941, when the station wagon and taxi were shifted to the passenger car line. Another minor

1937 Hudson/Terraplane Commercial Vehicles

Series	Body Style	Price	Weight	Wheelbase	Capacity
70	Utility coach	$725	2,685 pounds	117 inches	1/2 ton
70	Utility coupe pickup	$750	2,855 pounds	117 inches	1/2 ton
70	Cab pickup	$700	2,980 pounds	117 inches	3/4 ton
70	Panel delivery	$830	3,150 pounds	117 inches	3/4 ton
70	Station wagon	$905	3,060 pounds	117 inches	3/4 ton
70	Chassis and cab	$670	2,445 pounds	117 inches	3/4 ton
70	Chassis only	$570	2,080 pounds	117 inches	3/4 ton
Big Boy					
78	Cab pickup	$740	3,080 pounds	124 inches	3/4 ton
78	Custom panel delivery	$880	3,210 pounds	124 inches	3/4 ton
78	Chassis and cab	$700	2,540 pounds	124 inches	3/4 ton
78	Chassis only	$600	2,170 pounds	124 inches	3/4 ton

facelift was performed for 1942, but the war-shortened run accounted for a mere 67 commercial units.

After the war, the only Hudson commercial vehicle to return to production was the cab pickup. It was the same as the 1942 Big Boy 3/4-ton pickup with the new passenger car grille design.

Available records do not break down Hudson commercial model production by body style. Of the 8,058 commercials shipped in calendar year 1937, 950 are believed to have been Big Boy pickups and panels. How many of the remaining 7,000-plus units were utility coupe pickups is unknown.

Bill Hinde, who owns this 1937 Terraplane utility coupe pickup, knows of only one other 1937 and one 1938 registered with the Hudson-Essex-Terraplane Club. The owner of a boat dealership and automotive repair shop in

Above: Small loads get swallowed up in regular trunk. **Left:** *Flathead six was good for nearly 100 bhp.* **Below:** *No-frills steering wheel could have come from a pickup.* **Bottom:** *Simple grab handles move box in and out.*

Wichita, Kansas, Hinde has been "playing with Hudsons since 1941. My first one was a 1934 four-door Terraplane Six, a beautiful car. I was 15. I drove it too hard and wrecked it a couple times."

After serving in World War II, Bill bought a 1938 Hudson, which he drove on his honeymoon to Colorado, and later traded for a 1942 model. "I've had Hudsons continuously since then," he said, "probably a hundred or so. A lot of them were salvaged for parts." Only a couple of years ago he retired a 1950 Commodore bought in 1958. Besides the utility, he now owns a 1937 Hudson Eight found in a western Kansas wheat field in 1972 and a 1947 Commodore Eight four-door sedan.

The utility coupe pickup was sold new from Kingman, Kansas. A previous owner rescued it from a salvage yard and had Bill overhaul the engine and perform the service work on it during the ten years he owned it. It was also repainted the original black and re-upholstered with a straw and black patterned woven cloth that nearly duplicates the original material.

When his customer decided to sell the

rare coupe, Bill Hinde was first in line to buy it. The plain coupe makes a great companion for the luxurious 1937 and 1947 sedans — and the telescoping pickup bed in the trunk even comes in

handy for occasional light duty hauling for his shop. 🙠

Acknowledgments and Bibliography

Butler, Don, The History of Hudson; *Gunnell, John A.,* Standard Catalog of American Light Duty Trucks; *Kimes, Beverly Rae, and Clark, Henry Austin, Jr.,* Standard Catalog of American Cars, 1805-1942; *Brown, Arch, "Two-In-One Terraplane," Cars & Parts, December 1983; Williams, Bill, "1936 Terraplane driveReport," Special Interest Autos #12, August-September 1972; 1937 Hudson-Terraplane sales literature provided by Charles Liskow of the Hudson-Essex-Terraplane Club, Inc.*

Special thanks to Bill Hinde, Wichita, Kansas.

Comparison of 1937 Coupes with Trunk-mounted Pickup Boxes

Make	Wheelbase	Weight	Horsepower	Price
Terraplane	117 inches	2,855 pounds	96	$750
Plymouth	112 inches	2,700 pounds	82	$533*
Chevrolet	112.25 inches	2,770 pounds	85	$644*
Pontiac Deluxe 6	117 inches	3,165 pounds	85	$806*
* Business coupe with optional removable pickup box				

Working Willys
The plain, simple and cute 1938 Model 38 pickup

By John F. Katz
Photography by Vince Wright

The mid-summer corn stretches green and tall to either side as the little Willys pickup gently meanders the county highways, bumping and bouncing from field and farm to the final uphill grunt before the old general store. It isn't hard to imagine this charmingly basic truck working these same Pennsylvania farms some 60 years ago, pulling hay trailers, carrying crops to market, or hauling seed and supplies back home. But a lot of farms are for sale these days, and the general store is being renovated as a bed-and-breakfast. Up on I-78, the big trucks average 70-75 mph. And it *is* hard to imagine how the Willys would cope with the faster pace of modern traffic.

Knocked down by the Depression, Willys-Overland bet its future on small and simple vehicles that it could engineer, manufacture, and sell *cheap*, undercutting the Big Three not only on initial purchase price but maintenance costs as well. One Willys ad from 1937 tallied every conceivable economy afforded by a small four-cylinder car, beginning with the obvious frugality in gas, oil, tires, and depreciation and adding in less obvious savings, including fewer spark plugs to buy, fewer valves to grind, fewer piston rings to replace, fewer pounds of grease to pack into the smaller transmission and rear axle. Counting up the pennies, the ad ostensibly demonstrated how the Willys owner saved

enough money in 18 months to buy himself another new Willys!

It was an argument that should have appealed to the commercial market, where purchasing decisions usually fall to the guardians of the bottom line. Our driveReport truck, a 1938 model, offered a full-size, six-foot bed and a 1,000-pound carrying capacity; yet it rode on the shortest wheelbase, and was powered by nearly the smallest engine of any half-ton truck made in America.

To do that, however, something had to give, and the first thing that gave was passenger comfort. The Willys cockpit is so cramped I almost feel as though I've poured myself into a child's pedal car. The seat cushion is short and low, and the backrest thin and upright. The steering wheel rubs hard at my shirt, chiding me for wanton years of beer and pizza.

One Willys ad said that "the deep-cushioned seat is easily adjustable," but the bench in this truck is bolted solid to the floor. There wouldn't be any room to adjust it, anyway. Willys also claimed ample room for three across, but you couldn't slip Kate Moss into the space between owner John Haring and me, not even with a whole can of Wolf's Head.

The painted-metal dashboard houses the instruments low and in the center, diverting the driver's eyes far from the road ahead. There's a large speedometer on the right, and an equally large pod

containing amp, oil, and fuel gauges on the left. A small, round temperature gauge nestles between them, as if someone had initially forgotten it. (Someone had; it isn't there on '37 models.) The driver's sun visor hides the overhead wiper switch, but the remaining accessory controls—starter, choke, throttle, and lights— are clearly labeled and reachable at the bottom of the dash. The tiny rearview mirror doesn't quite cover the full width of the rear window, and with no side mirrors, the most reliable way to check behind you is to poke your head out of the side window and turn around.

The weather was brutally hot on the day of our drive, and the engine wouldn't start until John fiddled the choke and throttle into precisely the right positions. Once it fired, the engine's idle was busy, fast, and loud, with an industrial clatter somehow suitable for a working vehicle. John shouted that the valves have to be set hot, and so they are terrifically noisy before they warm up.

The handbrake rotates to release, and the engine noise subsides briefly as the clutch engages—only to rise louder, faster, and more intense than ever as the Willys accelerates in first gear. Now the gearbox howls as well. The throttle pedal doesn't move very far between all the way closed and all the way open, but that hardly matters; with only 48 horses under the hood, I pretty much used full throttle all the time.

The gear lever grazed reverse with a sharp clang as I pushed it ahead out of first and swung right for second. Otherwise, the Willys gearbox shifts pretty slickly for its time, with short throws and reasonably quick action—once I found its natural rhythm. Shift up into third before you reach 25 mph, and it practically puts itself in gear. Left there, the Willys can slow to the pace of a brisk walk and then slowly claw its way back up to speed; but the gearbox works so well you *want* to use it, if only to give the overworked engine every possible advantage. Drop below 20, and you can slip back into second with no double-clutching and just a momentary *graunch*. The helically cut second gear and direct-drive third turn considerably quieter than first.

Meanwhile, however, the long-stroke four thumps and rages like a tornado blowing about 200 marbles around inside a coffee can. The windshield wiper, dangling in my peripheral vision, wiggles distractingly. John said he's never pushed the truck over 40, and I didn't, either.

Willys vehicles were notorious for bump steer, and even minor pavement pimples sent our driveReport truck darting off in various directions. The steering is quick but loose, and corrections are difficult to judge. As with most trucks, however, its stiff chassis keeps it relatively flat in the corners, while pronounced understeer safely scrubs off speed. The stout springs bounce over bumps, but the strong, tubular shocks quickly snuff out any oscillations. It's no Cadillac, to be sure, but even on the worst surfaces the Willys never whacks its passengers really hard.

John worries about the brakes, but they are probably no worse than most others from the same era. Treated with respect, they perform adequately for the Willys' 35mph cruising speed. We did notice that they pull left once warmed up. The Willys certainly keeps its driver busy: shifting, steering, and correcting, all while crammed into about as much space as a computer tower leaves under a discount-store desk. That fragile-looking hood ornament, always looming in your view, suggests a grace and serenity that the Willys never achieves.

Yet the Willys retains a kind of ugly-duckling appeal, its rugged and functional simplicity suggesting a bigger, tougher, Midwestern-American 2CV. Even its oddball styling grows wistfully winsome with familiarity. Photographer Vince Wright thought it looked "peaceful," in marked contrast to the gratuitously aggressive design (and marketing image) of today's light trucks. Modern passenger-car styling, on the other hand, seems to strive for the harmonious and organic, with minimal brightwork; Willys was already there, 60 years ago, and with more individuality and character.

More to the point, the Willys was engineered to do a job, and that job was to haul 1,000 pounds of stuff at minimal expense. A second-hand Ford might have

carried as much, faster, and with less inconvenience to the driver; but Toledo offered a brand-new truck for 10 percent less than they were charging in Dearborn, or Warren, or Highland Park. Understand that, and you grasp the Willys completely.

Free the Willys

In 1928, Willys ranked third among U.S. automakers, with production of 314,500 units. No doubt the men of Toledo savored this victory, having struggled for half a decade to recover from ill-advised over-expansion just before the post-World War I recession.

To appease the banks, John North Willys had even temporarily surrendered control to Walter P. Chrysler. Now Chrysler had moved on to revive and rename Maxwell-Chalmers, and Willys enjoyed a comfortable confidence in his own company's future. In the summer of 1929, JNW sold his common stock in Willys-Overland for $21 million. The market crashed in October, but the infectiously optimistic Willys believed it would quickly recover. In March 1930 he embarked on a new career as the first U.S. ambassador to Poland.

Twenty-six months later, President Hoover asked Willys to resign his ambassadorship and return to Toledo, to save Willys-Overland one more time.

Willys management had not been idle in his absence. Since late 1931, they had been developing the Model 77, an evolutionary descendant of the compact and successful Whippet of 1927. JNW heartily endorsed their plan to discontinue all other models and to focus on the economy market.

Willys bodies were supplied by Murray, and Murray designer Amos Northup created the 77's somewhat controversial lines, mating a narrow passenger section to a sharply sloping hood and steeply raked-back radiator grille. The curvy 77

coupe exuded a rubber-duck cuteness that didn't translate well into the boxier sedan. (Northup also designed a scaled-up, six-cylinder Model 99, and while most sources say that tooling for this car was never completed, it now appears that 15 were actually built before management abandoned even this Model 77 variant.)

Regardless of how it looked, the 77 slipped through the wind credibly well, reaching an honest 71 mph on just 48 bhp. At Muroc dry lake in California, a stock 77 sedan averaged 65.5 mph in a 24-hour dependability run. Road racers soon recognized the 77's performance. Stripped-down 77's piloted by Barron Collier and Langdon Quimby challenged, and sometimes bettered, not only MG's and Lancias but Bentleys and even Bugattis in ARCA competition. A few 77-based specials were still racing as late as 1955.

Most 77 buyers were probably more impressed with the smoothness of its "floating power" engine mounts, which Walter Chrysler allowed JNW to use. And at just $375 for the four-door sedan, the 77 undercut Ford by $135. Among U.S.-built automobiles, only the $315 American Austin sold for less. But Willys-Overland had already lost $35 million between 1929-32, and production ceased on February 15, 1933, as the company slid into receivership.

The bankruptcy court allowed Toledo to produce two limited batches of 77s in 1934, probably fewer than Willys could have sold, even in those times. Undaunted, JNW sought financing from Toledo advertising exec (and Willys veteran) Ward Canaday, while attorney George Ritter worked out a re-organization scheme. A 1935 facelift gave the 77 a more upright and conventional appearance, borrowing styling details from Buick and LaSalle. By the end of the year Willys' reorganization was complete, and the receivership was lifted in early 1936. Morale soared on the Toledo assembly

Rounded styling and good proportions make Willys pickups attract attention wherever they go.

Integrated headlamps were ahead of their time.

Two-in-one brake and license plate lamp.

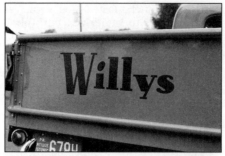

Non-original red letters used to match interior.

Deep bed can accommodate a sizable load.

line, and production tripled. But John North Willys didn't live to see it; he had passed away on August 26, 1935, at age 61. Bedridden, he worked on his company's reorganization until the end.

A significantly redesigned compact, the

TOTAL WILLYS PRODUCTION, 1933-42

Year	Production	Comments
1933	12,820	includes 15 Model 99's
1934	5,179	first run
	8,000	second run
	13,179	total
1935	10,700	
1936	30,825	
1937	63,467	
1938	26,680	
1939	2,624	Willys Model 48
	15,214	combined Willys and Overland Model 39
	17,838	total
1940	32,340	
1941	30,100	
1942	11,910	including military staff cars

SPECIALISTS

Willys World
George Romond
P.O. Box 5466
Dept. SIA-185
Plainfield NJ 07060

Ron Ladley
The Willys Man
1850 Valley Forge Rd.
Lansdale, PA 19446
Dept. SIA-185
610-584-1665

Don Crouthamel
Ol' 55 Chevy Parts/East Coast Chevy Inc.
4154 Skyron Drive
Dept. SIA-185
Doylestown, PA 18901
215 348-5568

Model 37, replaced the 77 in November 1936. Northup had come back with another bold and innovative design. The sedan resembled a short and chubby 810 Cord, while the more unique lines of the coupe flowed in undulating curves that began at the top of the windshield and slithered all the way down to the rear bumper. The front end showed Cord influence as well, in that it had no grille per se but instead a stack of horizontal louvers, a few of which flowed back almost to the front doors. But rather than copying the Cord's coffin-like snout, Northup gently rounded the Willys' front like the nose of an airplane or the prow of a ship. The headlights were set wide apart, in the tops of the fenders, with little speedlines behind them that echoed the louvers in the sides of the hood. If the arrangement suggested a Pierce-Arrow, well, Northup had begun his career in Buffalo. In overall effect, however, the Willys' face more closely resembled a gentler (and less costly) version of the sharknose Graham, which Northup also

WHAT TO PAY

Low	Average	High
$1,500	$6,000	$12,000

PROS & CONS

Pros
Distinctive looks that are very unique.
If you can find one, they're cheap to buy.
Attracts more attention than a Chevy pickup.

Cons
Build quality very suspect.
Rides like a hardtail Harley.
Body and trim parts hard to locate.

designed around the same time.

Willys ads billed the 37 as "the surprise car of the year" and "an engineering masterpiece." Although it retained the 77's 100-inch wheelbase, the Model 37 was longer, lower, and wider—by nearly a foot, an inch and a half, and almost eight inches, respectively. The front seat now measured 50 inches across, and tread width grew from 51 inches all around to 55 in the front and 58 in the rear. All-new, all-steel bodies averaged about 180 pounds heavier than their predecessors.

Mechanically, the 37 superficially resembled the 77, but only the engine and driveline had been carried over unchanged. The 37 chassis was stronger; it rode on smaller, 16-inch wheels and featured direct-acting tubular shock absorbers. Sales more than doubled over the already impressive record of 1936. By that time, however, Northup too, was gone, having died of head injuries after slipping on an icy sidewalk in February.

Willys go to work

After the bankruptcy of 1933, Willys no longer kept production records of individual body styles, or even separated passenger cars from commercial vehicles. Some sources have suggested that production numbers were intentionally fudged during the receivership of 1933-36. Willys expert Ron Ladley supplied the yearly totals listed on this page. He gleaned them from factory records and believes them to be accurate.

We do know that Willys produced more four-door sedans than anything else. Trucks were a sideline, with just 1,122 U.S. registrations in 1937—although many more could have been exported.

Willys had produced commercial vehicles under its own name since 1913, and had offered Overland trucks before that. But the first Willys product that we would recognize today as a pickup debuted as part of the Whippet range in late 1926. Rated (probably optimistically) for a half-ton load, it evolved parallel to the Whippet passenger car, adding a six-cylinder option in 1928. A bigger, Willys-badged pickup joined the line in 1930. Then both trucks vanished, along with the rest of the old Willys line, when Toledo decided to bet the farm on the new Model 77.

Initially, the only commercial version of the 77 was a panel van. A Willys pickup reappeared with the re-styled '35 models, although the light Model 77 frame limited its realistic carrying capacity to a quarter ton.

The 1937 Model 37 was also offered in both pickup and panel variations, but its sturdier frame allowed a true half-ton capacity. Like the 77 before it, the Model 37 pickup shared its front-end sheet metal with the corresponding passenger car, the cab even using a modified a sedan door. The Model 37 truck's rear fenders were unique, however, and much simpler in design than the passenger cars'.

The least expensive Willys truck was the "economy pickup," which sold for under $500. Except for eight-leaf springs in the rear, its chassis was identical to a Willys passenger car's, and its load capacity was limited to 750 pounds. The "Half-Tonner" cost $530, and added a heavy-duty Salisbury rear end and two-stage rear springs, packing ten leaves each. Its standard axle ratio was 4.7:1, which took a surprising bite out of performance, relative to the 4.3:1 gears installed in the passenger car and economy truck. Even shorter ratios of 4.9 and 5.1:1 were optionally available.

Steering was geared slower than in the car and the economy truck, too. Standard tires were still 5.50 x 16, but for the half-ton these were mounted on 4-inch rather than 3-1/2-inch rims. The larger rims could accommodate optional 6.00 x 16 tires, which in turn gave nearly nine inch-

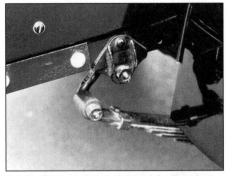

Semi-elliptic leaf springs used front and rear.

All controls are within easy reach of driver.

es of ground clearance. In addition to the pickup and panel van, Willys now cataloged a stake body, plus bare chassis, chassis-and-cab, and chassis-and-cowl configurations for the half-ton model.

"The new Willys Half-Tonner cuts costs...increases profits," boasted the trade-magazine ads. "Willys will do your half-ton delivery jobs speedily, dependably and at far less cost." The Willys promised not only economy in fuel, tires, and "upkeep," but also maneuverability "in traffic and in small places." The 750-lb-capacity "economy pick-up...brings

WHOLLY TOLEDO

People who are serious about preserving Willys use the serious pronunciation—"Willis"—which is how John North Willys said his name. Drag racers and street rodders seem to prefer the more playful "Willies." John Haring considers the latter an affectionate nickname, no different in principle from calling a Chevrolet a "Chevy."

John hung up his drag-racing helmet in 1979, and began looking for a '33 Willys panel van to rebuild as a street rod. Instead, he found our driveReport truck for sale at a speed shop in Delaware. It was wearing a 1966 Pennsylvania inspection sticker and had apparently served as a work truck until that time. Modern big-truck-style turn signals sprouted from the front fenders, and the headlight pods had been sawed off to accommodate sealed-beams, which were shoddily attached with sheet-metal screws. Virtually all of the original wiring was gone. But as shabby as the truck looked, it still had its original engine and an apparently honest 65,000 miles on the clock. The original spare tire, jack, and tools were with it, also.

The truck wasn't exactly what John wanted, but it was too complete to pass up. He still favored rodding over restoration until he spoke with Willys authority Ron Ladley. "I got educated about Willys and found out that wouldn't be a good idea," John told us. Ladley convinced him that a vehicle as original—and rare—as this pickup deserved to be restored to stock condition.

"An awful lot of compact Willys have survived," Ladley told us, "but not too many in original form. Back in the early Sixties, they went to race cars. That's how I got started with them, in '61, pulling them out of the woods and rebuilding them as racers. So many went to race cars and then were resurrected as street rods."

When John bought it, the Willys wore a coat of dull orange on its body and black on its fenders. Clearly, it was not original, and John decided to re-paint the truck an authentic Willys gray, which would have come with red pinstripes. He picked red upholstery to match the stripes. The Willys name painted on the tailgate should have been white, regardless of the truck's color, but John thought it looked better in red to match the seat and the stripes. Unable to find the correct color for the engine, he painted it an arbitrary black. He has a spare engine that's painted blue-green, but

isn't sure that that color is authentic, either.

The truck was found with the optional rear bumper and wheel trim rings. It had no factory radio or heater, although some previous owner had clumsily cut the firewall to install an incorrect heater. John decided not to put the trim rings back on, and added a right-side taillight, bumper guards, and 6.00 x 16-inch white-wall tires—all authentic options. Willys also offered dual side mirrors, dual windshield wipers, and dual sun visors, but John's truck has none of these.

The four-year restoration was a family project, involving John's wife Ellen and their children Scott, Tim, and Kristen. "We put it together a couple of times," John recalled. "Every winter they would dismantle some part of the truck, and try to have it back together in time to use it in the summer. Ladley supplied NOS hubcaps and door handles and reproduced the wiring harness and other small parts.

"Then in 1983," John recalled, "we ripped it apart real early. We had everyone lined up to do the sand-blasting and the painting." The sheet metal was restored by Don Crouthamel, who now works for a Doylestown Chevy supplier called Ol' 55. To save the original front fenders, Crouthamel welded metal rings to the sawed-off headlight pods, and then worked them back to their original shape. "And then we got it back together," John continued. "It's bad news to leave a car apart; the longer you leave them apart, the more problems you have putting them together." He and his family reassembled the Willys in time for that summer's "Das Awkscht Fescht" in Macungie. The truck won its First Junior at an AACA event in Cherry Hill, New Jersey, in 1986, picked up its Senior at Valley Forge in '87, and has collected a dozen Preservation awards since then. Just last summer, it returned to Cherry Hill for its first national award.

Willys engineering could be, ah, unique. The electrical system has no voltage regulator, just a cut-out switch. We noticed that keeping the hand throttle out just a little while idling keeps the ammeter from drifting into the discharge range. Insert-style main bearings support the crankshaft, but the rods ride on poured babbitt, limiting maximum engine speed to 3,200 rpm.

Fortunately, some parts from the more plentiful "Americar" fours will fit these earlier engines. The

'38 models came with a Tillotson carburetor that John described as "junk"; when Toledo switched to a Carter in 1940, the factory issued a retro-fit kit for earlier models, and John's truck has one of these.

The "eyeball"-style headlights insert from inside the fender, fastened only by a strap that clips, and the top is secured by a visible screw at the bottom. There is no bright bezel to mask a less-than-perfect fit, just a thin rubber gasket. This kind of desperate cost-cutting is evident throughout the vehicle. The inner door panels are made of a cardboard-like material and secured with visible plastic buttons. The brake and clutch pedals work from a common pivot, and if both are not correctly adjusted, the clutch pedal applies the brake. Rain water pools in the channels at the side of the cowl, where the hood closes, and unless this area is wiped dry with a towel, it rusts with astonishing speed. The pop-up cowl vent lacks a screen. And the truck's harsh ride will actually crack the front hood and fenders.

Inexplicably, Willys used two different styles of front fenders in '37-38. Both were fabricated from two separate stampings. In one type, the fender itself is one stamping and the headlight pod the other, and they are joined by a visible seam. John has a spare pair like this, but the fenders on his truck are of the other style, where the front and rear sections of the fender were stamped separately, with the headlight pod integral with the forward stamping. The two sections were butt-welded and ground smooth on the outside, although the seam remains visible underneath. Once assembled and painted, the two styles appear identical, except for the location of the seams.

John admits that he misses the modern amenities of a modified car. He won't take the Willys out after dark because of its exceedingly dim lights, and even in daylight, the truck's marginal performance and weak brakes discourage him from driving it on public roads. On the other hand, he allowed that "it's nice having a unique car. I take it to Hershey, and it's the only one there. And people from all over the United States love it.

"But it's 19 years later, and I still don't have my Willys street rod!"

Three-in-one oil, fuel and amp meter gauge.

Stylish speedometer tops out at 80 mph.

Basic bench seat reupholstered in red vinyl.

Plain inner door panels made of cardboard.

the big saving of the Willys principle of economy to hundreds of businesses where light delivery is required." Stake, canopy top, stock rack, grain box, and public utility bodies were "obtainable," and Willys entertained many custom orders. "Their production was so low," remarked Gordon Lindahl of The Willys Club, "that if someone came to them with a special purpose, they could do it—for 200, 100, or even 50 copies." Willys also offered PTO's, governors, and a wide range of truck accessories.

The 1938 Willys, which debuted on September 20, 1937, was renamed the Model 38, but differed very little from the Model 37. The speed lines disappeared from the headlight pods, but an elegant, almost fragile stand-up ornament appeared on the hood. Drip rails, seen only on Willys passenger cars in '37, were

added to trucks. Regardless, 1938 was bad year for everybody, and combined production of Willys cars and trucks shrank back down to 26,680. The *Standard Catalog of Light-Duty Trucks* reports that 1,889 of those were commercial vehicles, but Ladley doubts the accuracy of that figure.

More importantly, 1938 marked the arrival at Willys of Delmar G. "Barney" Roos, former SAE president and Studebaker engineer. Roos took over as chief engineer and immediately set about improving both performance and reliability.

The Willys lineup expanded again for '39, with the brief return of the Overland name. The new Model 39 featured fashionably squared-off headlights and a sharper, reverse-angle grille with even stronger Graham overtones. Hydraulic brakes arrived as well. Both standard and deluxe versions were produced with either Willys or Overland badges, with no apparent difference between them other than the name. Besides these, Willys also offered the less costly Model 48, with mechanical brakes and carryover styling from 1937-38. All Model 48s were Willys, and all '39 Willys pickups were Model 48s—essentially identical to the trucks produced in '37 and '38.

Then, as suddenly as it had arrived, the badge-engineered Overland vanished for 1940, and with it the eccentric styling of the past several years. The '40 Willys sported a neat and handsome look that would endear it to generations of drag racers and street rodders. Trucks caught up to cars with current sheet metal, although they retained cable brakes until '41.

It was in fact a truck that would shape Willys' destiny, but a different truck altogether. In August 1941, the Quartermaster General ordered 16,000 quarter-ton, four-wheel drive "general purpose" trucks from Willys. Soldiers would nickname them "Jeeps"—and for a while at least, the little company's future was assured. ❧

COMPARISON OF 1938 HALF-TONS

	Willys	Ford 60	Ford 85	Plymouth	Chevrolet	Dodge	GMC	IHC D5	IHC D2	Hudson	Studebaker
Price	$530	$580	$590	$585	$592	$600	na	na	na	$671	$850
Cylinders	4	V-8	V-8	6	6	6	6	4	6	6	6
Bore x Stroke	3.12 x 4.38	2.6 x 3.2	3.06 x 3.75	3.12 x 4.38	3.31 x 4.00	3.38 x 4.06	3.44 x 4.12	3.25 x 4.00	3.31 x 4.75	3.00 x 4.12	3.31 x 4.38
CID	134	136	221	201	207	218	230	133	213	175	226
Compression	5.7:1	6.6:1	6.12:1	6.7:1	6.0:1	6.5:1	na	na	6.3:1	6.5:1	6.0:1
Valve gear	L-head	L-head	L-head	L-head	OHV	L-head	L-head	L-head	L-head	L-head	L-head
Bhp	48 @ 3,200	60 @ 3,500	85 @ 3,800	70 @ 3,000	79 @ 3,200	75 @ 3,000	86 @ 3,600	33 @ 2,800	78 @ 3,400	83 @ 4,000	90 @ 3,400
Brakes	Mechanical	Mechanical	Mechanical	Hydraulic	Hydraulic	Hydraulic	Hydraulic	Hydraulic	Hydraulic	Hydraulic	Hydraulic
Wheelbase	100	112	112	112	112	116	112	113	113	112	116.5
Tires	5.60 x 16	6.00 x 16	6.00 x 16	6.00 x 16	6.00 x 16	6.00 x 16	6.00 x 16	5.25 x 18	various	5.50 x 16	6.00 x 16
Weight	2,226	2,526	2,684	na	2,805	2,700	na	na	na	2,750	3,250
Stroke/bore	1.40	1.23	1.22	1.40	1.21	1.20	1.20	1.23	1.44	1.37	1.32
Bhp/CID	0.36	0.44	0.38	0.35	0.38	0.34	0.37	0.25	0.37	0.47	0.40
Lb/Bhp	46.4	42.1	31.6	na	35.5	36.0	na	na	na	33.1	36.1

illustrations by Russell von Sauers, The Graphic Automobile Studio

© copyright 2001, Special Interest Autos

specifications

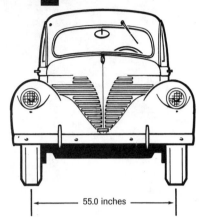

55.0 inches

100 inches

1938 Willys Model 38 half-ton pickup

Base price	$530
Std. equipment	Driver's side wiper and sun visor, 5.50 x 16 blackwall tires
Options on dR car	Rear bumper, front and rear bumper guards, dual taillights, 16 x 6.00 whitewall tires

ENGINE

Type	Four-in-line
Bore x stroke	3.125 inches x 4.375 inches
Displacement	134.2 cubic inches
Compression ratio	5.7:1
Horsepower @ rpm	48 @ 3,200
Torque @ rpm	100 @ 1,400-1,900
Taxable horsepower	15.6
Valve gear	L-head
Valve lifters	Mechanical
Main bearings	3
Induction	1 Carter 1-bbl downdraft
Fuel system	Mechanical pump
Lubrication system	Pressure
Cooling system	Pressure, centrifugal pump
Exhaust system	Single
Electrical system	6-volt

TRANSMISSION

Type	Warner three-speed manual, 2-3 synchronized
Ratios: 1st	2.43:1
2nd	1.426:1
3rd	1.00:1
Reverse	3.24:1

CLUTCH

Type	Borg & Beck single dry disc
Diameter	7.875 inches

REAR AXLE

Type	Salisbury, spiral-bevel
Ratio	4.7:1

STEERING

Type	Gemmer worm & gear
Ratio, gear	N/A
Turns lock-to-lock	N/A
Turning circle	34 ft. curb-to-curb

BRAKES

Type	Bendix "Duo-Servo" 4-wheel mechanical, cable actuated
Size, front	9-in. drum
Rear	9-in. drum
Lining area	134.9 square inches
Parking brake	Mechanical, on service brakes

CHASSIS & BODY

Construction	Ladder frame with 5 cross-members and cross-drilled XK-brace
Body	Welded steel stampings
Body style	2-seat pickup truck
Layout	Front engine, rear-wheel drive

SUSPENSION

Front	I-beam axle, semi-elliptic leaf springs
Rear	Live axle, semi-elliptic leaf springs

Shock absorbers, front	Tubular hydraulic
Rear	Tubular hydraulic
Wheels	Stamped steel disc, 16 x 4 in.
Tires	Allstate Safety Tread 6.00 x 16

WEIGHTS AND MEASURES

Wheelbase	100.0 inches
Overall length	175.5 inches
Overall width	69.8 inches
Overall height	N/A
Front track	55 inches
Rear track	58 inches
Approx. ground clear.	9 inches
Weight (empty)	2,226 pounds
GVW	3,350 lb.

CAPACITIES

Crankcase	4 quarts
Transmission (refill)	1.25 pints
Rear axle	1.25 pints
Cooling system	11 quarts
Fuel tank	8 gallons

CALCULATED DATA

Bhp/c.i.d.	0.36
Stroke/bore	1.40
Lb./bhp	46.4
Lb. per sq. in. (brakes)	16.5

Big wheel needed during slow-speed turns.

Inline L-head four makes 48hp at 3,200 rpm.

Single-barrel Carter downdraft supplies fuel.

Picking Up In Uruguay

by Alvaro Casal Tatlock
photos by the author

THERE is a paucity of pickup trucks in Uruguay, where I am managing director of the Automobile Club of Uruguay's museum in Montevideo. Hence, many older trucks are valued much more than the cars which are their contemporaries. Many cars are cut up to create utility vehicles; for these conversions, American automobiles are favorites because of their size and powerful engines.

I've taken a number of pictures recently of some of these conversions. All are in daily use, although some may seem to be falling to pieces. Usually police officers pretend not to notice that some of them would be unsafe at any speed, not having windshield wipers, adequate brakes or lighting equipment. ✍

Conversions range from the ingenious to the crude and are a tribute to the durability of older American cars. **Facing page, top and center:** '50 Pontiac before and after mechanical attention. **Bottom, left to right:** Scarce '52 Studebaker, tired '58 Chevy and '61 Ford "full size Ranchero." **Top left and right:** Who says Model A's aren't tough and adaptable? **Above center:** And the early V-8s are just as tough. **Above left:** In the US, Willys Americar would have become a dragster long ago. **Right:** Flight deck of '59 Chevy needed no conversion work. **Left:** This one started life as a "Plodge," an export '53 Plymouth with Dodge front end.

Pickup Clubs & Specialists

For a complete list of all regional pickup truck clubs and national clubs' chapters, visit **Car Club Central** at **www.hemmings.com**. With nearly 10,000 car clubs listed, it's the largest car club site in the world! Not wired? For the most up-to-date information, consult the latest issue of *Hemmings Motor News* and/or *Hemmings Collector Car Almanac*. Call toll free, 1-800-CAR-HERE, Ext. 550.

PICKUP TRUCK CLUBS

American Truck Historical Society
300 Office Park Dr.
Birmingham, AL 35223
205-870-0566
Dues: $25/year; Membership: 22,000

Antique Truck Club of America
P.O. Box 291
Hershey, PA 17033
717-533-9032
Dues: $25/year; Membership: 2,400

National Chevy/GMC Truck Association
P.O. Box 607458
Orlando, FL 32860
407-889-5549
Dues: $30/year

Scout & International Truck Association
P.O. Box 12
Ogden, IL 61859

United Scouts & Association USA
3369 Sugar Pike Rd.
Canton, GA 30115

SPECIALISTS AND RESTORERS

Mack Products
P.O. Box 856
Moberly, MO 65270
660-263-7444
Pickup bed parts 1928–72, most makes

Cheyenne Pickup Parts
Box 959
Noble, OK 73068
405-872-3399
Full-size Chevrolet pickup parts 1960–87

Mar-K Quality Parts
6625 W. Wilshire Blvd.
Oklahoma City, OK 73132
405-721-7945
Restoration and custom pickup parts

Bruce Horkey's Wood & Parts
46284 440th St.
Windom, MN 56101
507-831-5625
Ford, Chevy, GMC, and Dodge pickup parts

Obsolete Ford Parts, Inc.
8701 S. I-35
Oklahoma City, OK 73149
405-631-3933
Ford pickup parts

The Filling Station
990 South Second St.
Lebanon, OR 97355-3227
800-841-6622
Chevrolet and GMC truck parts, 1918–1972

Pickups Northwest
1430 Bickford Ave.
Snohomish, WA 98290
360-568-9166
1937–87 pickup parts

American Classic Truck Parts
PO Box 409
Aubrey, TX 76227
940-365-9786
1936–87 Chevrolet and GMC pickup truck parts

Chevy Duty
1 Chevy Duty Dr.
Kansas City, MO 64150
800-741-1678
Classic Chevy and GMC pickup parts

Classic Industries
18460 Gothard St.
Huntington Beach, CA 92647
800-854-1280
Chevrolet and GMC truck parts 1934–2001

The Truck Shop
P.O. Box 5035, Dept. 1
Nashville, GA 31639
229-686-3833
Chevy and GMC truck parts 1934–87

Ole Chevy Store
2509 S. Cannon Blvd.
Kannapolis, NC 28083
704-938-2923
1947–72 truck parts

Obsolete Chevrolet Parts Co.
P.O. Box 68
Nashville, GA 31639-0068
800-248-8785
1929–70 Chevy truck parts

Year One
P.O. Box 129
Tucker, GA 30085-0129
800-430-9840
1967–87 Chevrolet and GMC truck parts

Jim Carter Classic Truck Parts
1508 East Alton
Independence, MO 64055
800-336-1913
1934–72 Chevrolet and GMC truck parts

Golden State Parts
3493 Arrowhead Dr.
Carson City, NV 89706
714-441-0200
1947–87 Chevy and GMC truck parts

H&H Classic Parts
12325 Hwy. 72 W.
Bentonville, AR 72712
479-787-5575
1955–72 Chevrolet truck parts

Brothers
4375 Prado Rd. #105
Corona, CA 92880
800-977-2767
1947–72 Chevrolet and GMC truck parts

LMC Truck
P.O. Box 14991
Lenexa, KS 66285-4991
800-222-5664
Chevrolet and Ford truck parts

Chev's of the 40's
2027 B Street, Dept. 1A,
Washougal, WA 98671
800-999-2438
1937–54 Chevy truck parts

Roberts Motor Parts
17 Prospect St.
West Newbury, MA 01985
800-231-3180
Dodge truck parts

Concours Parts and Accessories
3493 Arrowhead Dr.
Carson City, NV 89706
888-600-7278
1948–66 Ford truck parts and accessories

Dennis Carpenter
4140 Concord Parkway So.
Concord, NC 28027
800-476-9653
Ford truck parts